LEADERSHIP AND CONSCIOUSNESS

The Three-Ring Model for Integrating
Personal and Business Growth

FEDERICO RENZO GRAYEB

Foreword by Ken O'Donnell

Praise for *Leadership and Consciousness*

"In our challenging times when sustainability depends on new models of economics and leadership and, decision making is becoming ever more decentralized, there is an impending need for a new business consciousness. Mr. Grayeb's book has the quality of being grounded in the entrepreneur world while bridging with wider aspects of what business ultimately represents, namely the arena of life's exchanges. A book from within the corporate world, written in its language and jargon with a spiritual flair that will have you reflecting on the way you impact this world."

—Rabbi Nilton Bonder
Spiritual leader and author of Our Immoral Soul

"In this book, Federico appeals to the restlessness of executives who want to feel and express things more consciously but are caught in the productive machine. The book reflects the search for deeper answers to why we do what we do and if we really need to run around so much."

—Ken O'Donnell
Author and Organizational Consultant
Fellow, Oxford Leadership Academy

"The transformation of business starts by transforming people. Leaders with an integral vision, who truly understand interdependence and live with this notion, will cause a profound change in society. *Leadership and Consciousness* invites us to fully develop the potential of individuals. Once more aware and happier, they will connect among themselves for a greater common purpose"

—Alessandro Carlucci
President and CEO
Natura Cosméticos S.A.

"As I read through this book, I was moved by the holistic approach that Federico applies to business, unifying the personal and group aspects of any business with community interaction. Social responsibility is a crucial ingredient to our survival as a species—economic and otherwise. No longer is it enough to "teach a man to fish"—we must teach others (children and adults) the social and emotional skills necessary to become successful. Grayeb takes us through a journey to understand these truths in a work that is brilliant in its simplicity and depth."

—Yossef Sagi
Spirituality for Kids International, Inc.

"The biggest challenge of a leader is to maintain a deep connection with the base of the organization. The vision or purpose of a leader needs to get down to the *shop floor*, and for that, he or she needs to cultivate habits that will create the company's culture. These habits depend on a strong leadership. That is one of the biggest challenges we leaders face. This book helps with a structured approach to understanding the levels of consciousness, which will lead to stronger connections between stakeholders and higher chances for a leader to succeed."

—Thomas Eckschmidt
Cofounder of PariPassu

LEADERSHIP AND CONSCIOUSNESS

The Three-Ring Model for Integrating Personal and Business Growth

FEDERICO RENZO GRAYEB

To those who lead by example.

ACKNOWLEDGMENTS

No book stands alone. Many people have influenced the shape and content of this project, and many more have supported me through it, from those who wrote the lyrics of favorite songs that inspired me to reflect on the message behind what I used to carelessly sing in my adolescent years to authors—ranging from the classics to contemporary philosophers. I have also had the immense privilege to have encountered incredible teachers, counselors, supervisors, and coaches in my professional life. They helped me understand the need to stop blaming the outside world for all of the ugly things I was seeing and turn that energy inward. Doing so started me on a path of personal and spiritual development through immersion into a deeper level of consciousness that permitted me to take action and actually *do* something about it.

I also want to thank Charles Patti for putting up with my bombardment of thoughts; his thoughtful and compassionate comments over so many years often helped me refine ideas and their expressions. I had the privilege of coming across extraordinarily generous and talented individuals who gave me intriguing insights and valuable suggestions, like Richard Greaves and professor Jose Luiz Tejon. Many other influences should be acknowledged, not the least of which is the inspiration of people who work to make a difference in this world, like my yoga teacher, Gonzalo Rico Peña, and social and religious leaders like Rabbis Sergio Bergman and Nilton Bonder. Many heartfelt thanks also go out to psychiatrist Angeles Moreno for her professional insight into the realm of the human mind.

I would like to make my final acknowledgment to my organizational psychologist and friend, Renato Spomberg, who has been an important backdrop to many of the key intellectual developments underlying this book, from conception to final delivery.

"Man surprised me most about humanity. Because he sacrifices his health in order to make money. Then he sacrifices money to recuperate his health. And then he is so anxious about the future that he does not enjoy the present, the result being that he does not live in the present or the future; he lives as if he is never going to die, and then dies having never really lived."

—The Dalai Lama

CONTENTS

FOREWORD

Public education has not varied much since the Industrial Revolution. The content and curricula, of course, have exploded as everything has become more and more complex, but the basic process of putting young people through an assembly-line type of educational system continues pretty much the same. Children start off in preschool and kindergarten, work their way through primary and secondary schools, and, if they are fortunate, make it on to universities. Hopefully, they can then make a contribution to the economic, social, and political system they are a part of and pay back the time, money, and energy that were dedicated to their training.

One of the roots of the word "educate" is *educere*, Latin for "to conduct outward." In other words, there is an inner potential in every student that needs to be recognized and developed from the inside out. The assembly-line approach to education builds itself almost entirely on available and functional information, from which we are expected to develop some useful skills for the system and possibly marketable know-how that can help us obtain and maintain jobs. Our own ability to learn defines the life and work experiences that help us develop conscious values and principles and lead us to wisdom. There is a divorce between the functional education that feeds the system and the practical education we need to develop our lives. That's why there is such a clear gap between the skills we practice as individuals and organizations and the lack of care that we show toward the planet and its future. We can send rockets to Mars, but we can't make sensible changes that allow our cities to function better. We learn complex mathematics but not necessarily the logic to live our lives. We learn grammatical rules, but we don't know how to communicate our real feelings.

In the so-called digital era, in which individual needs have become so personalized and customized, it is incredible that we continue to churn out batches of students who have not been taught how to think, speak, or act in a conscious way for the benefit of the whole. By and large, Henry

Ford (an American industrialist who founded the Ford Motor Company and who sponsored the development of the assembly-line technique of mass production) and Frederick Winslow Taylor (an American mechanical engineer who sought to improve industrial efficiency) are still the kings of the way we do the routine work necessary to keep the system alive. A little more than one hundred years ago, Taylor espoused his philosophy of management, which stated that, although man had been the first consideration in the past, in the future, the system must be first. In factories and offices all around the world, this, unfortunately, is still true.

In Ford's plants, people were considered to be as interchangeable and easily replaced as the raw materials they were working with. Ford said he did not want people who thought; he just wanted their hands. The term "human resources" still carries this connotation. In a congress on human resources in Rio a few years ago, Peter Senge, a senior lecturer in leadership and sustainability at the MIT Sloan School of Management, started off by defining the word "resource" as "something waiting to be used." He then asked the people in the audience how many of them worked in human resources. No one raised their hand.

It is no wonder that we develop great skills but not necessarily great spiritual and human awareness. We mass-produce many things to support the way we have decided to live our lives. Unfortunately, we also mass-produce people who are unaware, or maybe slightly aware, of the consequences of those decisions.

In the following excerpt from his poem "The Rock" (1934), T.S. Eliot expresses this very clearly:

The endless cycle of idea and action,
Endless invention, endless experiment,
Brings knowledge of motion, but not of stillness;
Knowledge of speech, but not of silence;
Knowledge of words, and ignorance of the Word.
All our knowledge brings us nearer to our ignorance,

All our ignorance brings us nearer to death,
But nearness to death no nearer to God.
Where is the Life we have lost in living?
Where is the wisdom we have lost in knowledge?
Where is the knowledge we have lost in information?

Working in companies in these frenetic times has become stressful, technological, and fast-paced—not exactly conducive to the nurturing of our innate spirituality and consciousness. The realities and demands of a volatile global market have totally transformed the way organizations relate internally and externally. Therefore, anything that can help us create healthy organizational cultures where human beings can do and be their best is welcome, as in this book by Federico. By making an excellent case for conscious leadership, he challenges current management models that are too rigid and insufficient for the challenges ahead. It is just not necessary for executives to reach unsustainable levels of stress in order to produce reasonable returns for shareholders. Conscious living and working is not counterproductive to the business ethic. It just means that we can think less and do better, and at the same time remain satisfied with ourselves and our jobs.

Because of the increasing oddities in the corporate world, there is a perceivable movement here and there toward a more meaningful and higher-quality life than monetary compensation, perks, or bonuses can provide. People want more control over their lives. It is not a matter of making a trade-off between life and work. It is about feeling more alive and energized and performing work consciously. After all, these days, work is where we spend up to fifty or sixty hours a week and more than a third of our lives.

Because of the increasing levels of complexity, no person is smart enough to make all of the decisions. Collective intelligence has to be developed and accessed so that the right responses to the enormous challenges can be made. This is why the command-and-control type of leader is reaching extinction. Such a person, if asked, would say that he wishes he could control other people, situations, and time. Of course that is impossible. A conscious leader understands that people and situations can grow and produce only if healthy conditions exist. Plants need soil, water, air, and light, as well as time and space to produce. It is useless to stand in front of the plants and shouting at them to grow.

In this book, Federico appeals to the restlessness of executives caught in the productive machine and who want to feel and express things more consciously. The book reflects the search in each of us for the reasons we do what we do and for the acknowledgment that perhaps we do not really need to run around so much. The title of the book, *Leadership and Consciousness*, leaves no doubt about its theme. The logic of self-awareness, team awareness, and community awareness holds it together excellently. He very cleverly connects meaning in our deeper selves with the work that we have to do with our teams. After all, we are leaders only if other people accept us as such. Our teams should feel happy with our presence and not celebrate our absence. If we are conscious at an individual level, we can understand others better and interact with them in a way that brings out the best in them as well. Obviously, if we are conscious about the meaning of our own lives and how they fit in the world in which we live, we will be proactive toward the community and environment around us.

Conscious leadership feeds the natural practice of values, especially with difficult people and adverse situations. After all, it's easy to be peaceful with our friends, but we also have to bring peace to our enemies.

Our previous education and formal training, as mentioned earlier, may have helped us swim well in more tranquil business atmospheres. Conscious leadership helps us swim in the heavy seas. We have to be more like surfers than pool swimmers. As surfers, we know we cannot control the sea or the other surfers. We can only be examples of the type of behavior we want to see in others. We know we do not determine the shape or the size of the waves, but we have the patience to choose the best ones, the agility to catch them, and enough balance to keep from falling.

Our goal is not to get to the beach, or even to get there before the other surfers. It is to derive the maximum benefit while the wave lasts.

The counterpoint to the "art of war," as preached to our MBA students, is actually the art of being relevant. In the permanent uncertainty in which we live, only those who are relevant will remain standing. A conscious leader has a greater chance of making the best decisions for the best results for the whole: self, team, organization, and community.

Federico Renzo's book on conscious leadership is a thoughtful reminder of what leaders or apprentice leaders need to aim toward.

—Ken O'Donnell
Fellow, Oxford Leadership Academy

PROLOGUE

Right after the 2008 financial crisis exploded, I was invited to participate in a conference panel at the Massachusetts Institute of Technology (MIT) on New Business Models in Latin America. The conference was targeted to MBA students from that university and others in the Boston area. While working on my speech, I was trying to decide which route to take.

One choice for my speech was to take the safest and most treaded path of traditional management speeches. I could start with a powerful opening, like "transformational leadership and your success," and then add phrases here and there, like "assessing organizational opportunities, implementing strategic excellence, revitalizing operational capabilities"— or any other random combination of these words. Then I could move into storytelling mode to describe the opportunities the emerging market presented to these ambitious students desperate to accelerate their progress by climbing the corporate ladder and achieving financial success.

Or I could take the riskier path, which would be to discuss *integral leadership*. At that time, I was working with an organizational psychologist on a new and more authentic approach to leadership, which, despite many obstacles at work, I was slowly trying to implement in my company. Deep inside, my greatest fear was that students would make fun of concepts such as self-awareness and conscious leadership—and, ultimately, of me. This conference offered me a unique opportunity to knock them dead and make a good impression at this highly prestigious school. I did not want to screw it up and be mocked as an aspiring New Age guru.

After some internal conflict, I decided to embrace my fears and arrive at the meeting with two different speeches: the traditional leadership speech and the holistic one. I would then decide which of the paths to take on the spur of the moment.

At the conference, two of us were on the panel, and the other person started his speech using many of the concepts related to the traditional mechanistic leadership model. When he was done, I decided to try the unexplored route of conscious leadership...I started speaking from deep down inside me, and it was the first time I experienced a power within me that translated into an extremely passionate speech (which was not how I usually behave at all!). I was pleasantly surprised at the reaction from the audience during and after the conference. I sincerely never would have expected such a high level of interest in an otherwise materialistic audience (that was, of course, not reality but just *my* prejudice). The looks on the faces of those students gave me the force to continue down that path, and that is the main reason why I started to write this book: I sincerely hope to convey, throughout these pages, the learning from all those years of personal and professional self-exploration from the experiences I have had as a leader in multinational companies. After so many years, I have found a purpose in what I do: to try to raise the self-awareness of business leaders so that, together, we can make a difference in our societies, in our lives, and in the lives of those who surround us.

I sincerely hope this book will help you find your own path toward deeper levels of consciousness, help you find your own purpose and sense of meaning, and instill in you the passion to lead others in an authentic way.

—Federico Renzo Grayeb

PART ONE

THE RINGS OF
CONSCIOUS LEADERSHIP

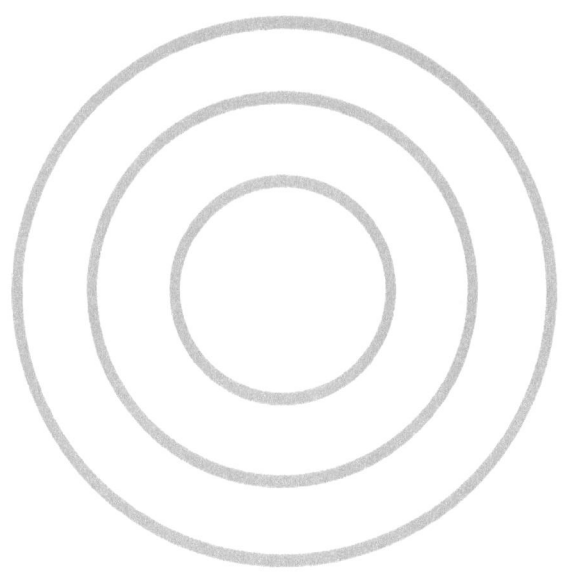

Chapter One

INTEGRATED LEADERSHIP TODAY

The greatest of faults is to be conscious of none.
—Thomas Carlyle

War on terror. Financial crisis. Systemic corruption. Economic meltdown. Labor unrest. Political instability. Civilian uprisings.

Every single day, we are constantly being bombarded with bad news from all imaginable places that reinforces the perception that the world is becoming a pretty unpleasant place to be in. One wonders when it will ever be possible to read the news and *not* be confronted with the word "crisis." Many of us are, indeed, experiencing the rapid deterioration of our external environment. We see problems popping up throughout the whole world and in several different arenas: political, societal, economic, etc.

Additionally, unlike previous world crises, this time it seems as if the world has not suffered just minor damage but has definitely become broken. It seems as if the negative effects of the present downturn are lasting much longer than previously anticipated—as if a historical paradigm shift may be occurring. The 2008 world financial crisis could be an example. Previously, we were used to experiencing economic peaks and valleys, but all were part of an upward trend. They were just minor or major distortions and statistical variances in the long-term growth of the global economy. But now something is different. Many years have already passed, and it seems as if we still are not able to see the light at the end of this tunnel—or will it be the light of another oncoming train? Every time it seems we are about to exit the tunnel, something new happens to make us dip again and end up in the same rut. Something has changed, but we still cannot grasp what it is exactly. All we know is that the old mechanistic approaches to solving economic crises do not seem to be working anymore. It appears as if we are not able to cope with such a hostile environment.

Bad news, however distant it may seem, is eroding our own certainties, and it may not be possible to recoil from the world's violence and misfortunes anymore. Sometimes we selfishly hope that all of this negativity will happen outside of our supposedly impenetrable cocoons. Unfortunately, it is just a mere illusion; we are all interconnected, and there is no way that the *external world* will not be able to penetrate our *internal* one; the external shakeouts are producing tremors that affect us and the people who are near and dear to us. It is not feasible to turn away from world events, to act as if what is going on *out there* has nothing to do with us. We are all actors in this play; we are all in the same boat. Every man carries in him the whole of the human condition.[1] Look around and honestly ask yourself if most of your friends and acquaintances are optimistic about their future, if they envision a peaceful world and a better place for future generations, and if they experience job stability in their companies and fair income distribution in their own societies. Most importantly, do you sense in them and in yourself a high level of *serenity and inner peace*?

Long-Held Beliefs that Are No Longer True

On top of that, for a very long time, we have lived with the illusion that life could be under control, that we would find ways to cope with uncertainty, and that we would be able to solve our issues with the same tried approaches. But now it seems that many of our assumptions were based on beliefs that do not hold water anymore. Here are some examples of formerly unquestionable assumptions:

- We believed in uninterrupted economic growth, economic cycles of peaks and valleys, unlimited resources, and the absence of consequences from human greed.
- We believed that somebody would be spared from this crisis. But the truth is, almost no nation, no company, no individual was unaffected. Businesses that were considered icons in their industry no longer exist. Safe havens have disappeared; even the most stable countries from the old—and once prosperous—world are now crumbling.
- We believed that the most advanced nations would behave in a more conscientious way, that—unlike the underdeveloped world or the emerging economies—they would not fall into the traps of demagogy, that they would not be that shortsighted, and that they would take the necessary preventive measures to deal with human greed and corruption and avoid long-term damage to society overall.

More specifically, in our own workplaces, the loss of the previously mentioned certainties is resulting in mood alterations among the people we lead. An increased level of fear, anxiety, and overall insecurity is paralyzing our employees and hampering the good qualities we need in them (creativity, common sense, and resilience), particularly during these chaotic times. Unless we invest time and resources in working on these issues—on personal development, on human relations, on improving the way our organizations interact with our communities—we, as leaders, will not be able to really *succeed*. (I do not mean "succeed" in a mere materialistic way but in broader, holistic terms. Later on, I will define true success and purpose in life.)

Now is the time for managers and company leaders to act and take responsibility to help society find a way out. As gloomy as the present external environment may seem, it also offers a unique opportunity to all of us. Things do not happen by chance, and I am a firm believer that we can make a quantum leap in our behaviors that will enable us and the people we lead to weather these and future storms during these times. We will never be able to control the external world, but we have the ability to actualize enormous hidden potential that is presently lying dormant in the universe. The change that we are all looking for depends on each one of us—on an *internal change* that needs to take place in our souls and hearts. It requires us not to make incremental changes but to *evolve* as human beings—to move beyond the problem-solving mentality into a *sense-making* one. We, as responsible business and community leaders, have the opportunity to detect the first waves of these paradigm shifts in our own organizations and, therefore, are bound by duty to do something about it.

I believe mankind has crossed a threshold and that life for us will not be the same again, nor will we be able to solve our issues with the same tried approaches. As Albert Einstein once said, "Problems cannot be solved at the level of awareness that created them."[2] Our overall low level of consciousness caused by systematic denial permitted such an absurd phenomenon as the subprime-mortgage bubble to happen. An equally low level of consciousness caused us to try to come up with solutions that (at least as of the day this book was published) are flat out not working. We need to realize that the problem is not only external but also much more deeply inward. We have to resolve the inward issues that cause these external phenomena. It all starts with *oneself*. The first step to take is to look at the way each of us lives our lives. As Thomas Hobbes wrote, "Whoever looks into himself shall know the thoughts and passions of all other men."[3]

My objective for this book is to discuss a holistic approach to leadership and to demonstrate the close link between personal and business development. My intention is to move away from the dissociated recipes of corporate slogans and methodologies that many business coaches preach based on symptomatic approaches. (One example is the infamous, flavor-of-the-month corporate workshops that produce more resentment among team members for the time lost than actual solutions to business matters, creating deep levels of frustration in our workforces by focusing on effects instead of causes.) This different model calls for us to place reflection first and action afterward. It has much more to do with *finding your life purpose* than attaining business goals, aiming for excellence in what you do rather than conquering mere achievements and experiencing pleasure rather than just having fun in what you do.

The Rings of Conscious Leadership

Imagine the developmental path of the conscious leader as three concentric rings, each representing a different level of awareness: of the self, of his or her work team, and of the community in which he or she interacts. In this book, I advocate for an *integrated leadership* model of these three rings through immersion into deeper levels of *consciousness*. It consists of a journey of discovery and increased awareness, first and foremost of the leader, then of the people he or she interacts with at work, and finally, of the external environment. The model calls for an integration of the dissociated parts of you as a person and leader and of your surroundings. You will need to dive into deeper levels of self-awareness, which will allow the inner ring to become stronger and larger, expanding its influence into the two outer rings, which refer to your people and to your world.

Self-awareness

Team-awareness

Community-awareness

In practical terms, the conscious leader needs to go through three steps to integrate the dissociated rings:

1. **Self-awareness ring**—The journey starts with the creation of a purpose, a deep meaning to your lives and jobs, a mission, and a personal realization that needs to go beyond material success. It then moves into increasing your level of consciousness, integrating more of what you say with what you actually *feel* and do, and integrating your internal and external aspects. That means integrating the objective aspects with the

subjective ones—thinking, sensing, intuition, and emotions. In other words, this ring stresses the value of a holistic approach to problems, whereby the whole individual is considered, not only his or her rational side.

2. **Team-awareness ring**—The objective here is to integrate your working teams and help team members increase their own level of consciousness. As soon as they believe deeply that their leader cares for them and clearly wants to look after their well-being as persons, team spirit and effectiveness will rise, creating a sense of belonging. If we share the same beliefs, if honest team spirit becomes a reality, if people really feel (not just say) that they are part of a team, then that is when actual team building takes place and team awareness surges.

3. **Community-awareness ring**—The journey continues with the integration of you and your employees with the community in which you operate. The goal is to increase the level of consciousness of our companies. This higher awareness of the external world will allow us to understand better how we are all interconnected and how our behavior and our companies' behaviors and actions can impact our surroundings. There is a dire need to rethink social responsibility initiatives—not as mere company branding but as an honest desire to give back to and interact with the communities we operate in and are interconnected with.

In this book, I will try to bring the concepts around the three rings of leadership to life with cases I have either experienced personally or heard from former colleagues. For the sake of confidentiality, I have altered names and/or unessential information.

PART TWO

THE SELF-AWARENESS RING

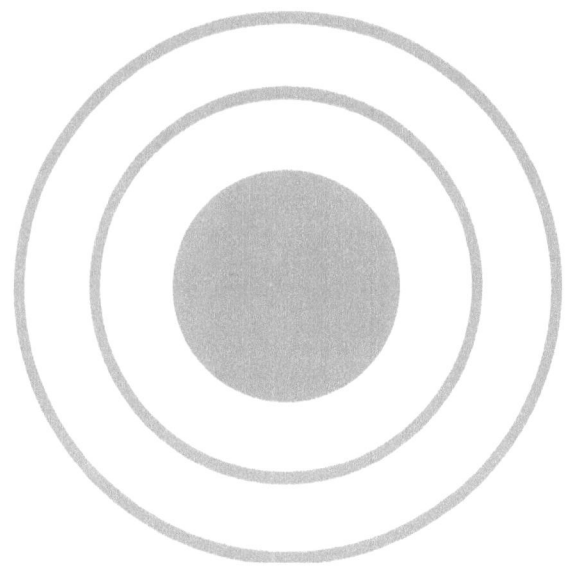

Chapter Two

GOALS AND PURPOSES

Well you told me one time that you'd be somebody
That you weren't workin' just to survive
But you're workin' so hard that you don't even know you're alive
Workin' so hard to be somebody special
Not working just to survive
Well, you're special to me, babe, but what I don't see, babe, is
Where you go once you arrive.
—Paul Williams, "Special to Me"

When I first met Richard, one of his major complaints was about his ever-demanding boss, who never seemed to be content with what Richard did. Yes, there were those empty praises, such as, "Terrific job!" and, "Well done!" and the like, but Richard perceived that they were delivered in the same tone and with the same facial gestures as when his supervisor would ask about the weather or the time. I once asked Richard *what* he worked for (I was afraid that asking about a purpose would paralyze him), and he remained speechless. After reframing my question into *whom* he worked for, he immediately responded, "My boss, of course!" Gone were the carefully worded company mission and the beautiful and moving statements about the importance of the company stakeholders, environment, and community.

Richard's objective was to please his boss by achieving increasingly demanding financial results in his area. This boss-pleasing strategy had proven to be successful in the past, and thanks to this fact, Richard always managed to move up in the organization. But it became harder and harder for him to become motivated, and boredom seemed to kick in much too

often. Something was missing in Richard's life, but what? It seemed that all of his achievements did not produce the energy to wake him up each morning, to push him further even when he was at his worst... The human flaws of laziness, frustration, and/or fatigue were kicking in, and Richard just could not find inspiration to get himself moving in a certain direction. At a one point, Richard could not continue hiding these feelings, and his team started to get dragged down by the same sentiments. Once the star of the company, he received a modest "meets expectations" rating on his year-end performance appraisal for the first time. Right afterward, during a business-review meeting with the executive committee, Richard sensed that he was no longer being appreciated and *celebrated* as he used to be, and he decided to hand in his resignation. Everybody was shocked to learn that it took so little to drive him to make such an abrupt decision. Why would such a clever guy with a history of so many successes make such a decision? Was it because his level of tolerance for constructive criticism and his resilience were low?

Absence of Purpose

A quote from the famous British writer Dorothy Sayers may fit very well into Richard's situation: "In the world it is called tolerance, but in hell, it is called despair; the sin that believes in nothing, cares for nothing, seeks to know nothing, interferes with nothing, enjoys nothing, hates nothing, finds purpose in nothing, lives for nothing, and remains alive because there is nothing for which it will die."[1]

Even though this may sound a little extreme for this case, it describes pretty well a sentiment that is pervading our society and, thus, many corporations: an extremely low level of resilience and tolerance when the first difficulties arise. Richard was not able to weather a single storm because he did not have any island to get to. His lack of purpose deprived him of the needed energy that would otherwise make him resilient to external criticism. His level of self-awareness was so low that he never honestly asked himself what his real work motivations were. This lack of inner meaning was compensated for by external factors that are as fragile as they are elusive: a friendly environment, constant positive reinforcement from his peers and boss, excellent business results, etc. The moment the external environment turned a little bit hostile (an average-performance appraisal rating, in his case), he realized that his work life was based on pillars of sand.

In *Man's Search for Meaning*, Viktor Frankl said, "What man actually needs is not a tensionless state but rather the striving and struggling for some goal worthy of him. What he needs is not the discharge of tension at any cost but the call of a potential meaning waiting to be fulfilled by him."[2] When he founded the Viktor Frankl Institute of Logotherapy based on his experiences in the Nazi death camps, Dr. Frankl discovered that people who had hope of being reunited with loved ones, projects they felt a need to complete, or great faith tended to have better chances than those who had lost all hope. During his ordeal, Dr. Frankl came into contact with people who, despite the extreme negative circumstances and expectations, managed to achieve inner peace and serenity. (And he was actually one of them!) In fact, one of the principles behind logotherapy is that man is a being whose main concern consists of fulfilling a meaning and actualizing values rather than merely gratifying and satisfying drives and instincts. There was no way prisoners in the death camps would have been able to find any gratification of their basic needs in such a horrendous environment.

The world is going through difficult times, but a death camp is, fortunately, an extreme example of a hostile external environment that we all hope will never, ever exist again. I wanted to use this image to depict the extent to which human beings are able to cope with awful negative circumstances when they have a clear purpose to fulfill. Companies are surely no death camps, nor do we necessarily need to look for transcendental meaning to our jobs, but unless we find a purpose in what we do, we will have many colleagues like Richard, whose motivations revolved around external effects that cannot be controlled. Richard's life was a pointless race toward bigger and bigger accomplishments, with pats on the back from the crowd saluting the runner but with no finish line in sight. Even if the final goal was actually to please somebody else (boss/family/friends), how would he ever be able to control other people's feelings? He could have surely provided better and better business results for the company, and still his boss may have never been satisfied for reasons beyond Richard's control.

The pervading reductionist vision in many management theories promotes the idea that people's motives usually boil down to just four items: money (getting a raise in salary), power (obtaining a coveted promotion), status (acquiring a more lofty company title), and popularity (a burning need to be liked by everyone). I am not against any of these, but I believe we human beings are much more complex and that living a mere *goal-centered life* is not sustainable, neither for the individual nor for society as a whole. We may achieve many goals that can make us happy or proud for a while, but like caffeine, this effect will peak and then subside, and then we will need more coffee to get us going (higher salary, bigger office, job promotion, etc.)...until we are suffering from ulcers!

The Difference between Goals and Purposes

In our jobs, we have many goals to achieve, but these cannot be considered purposes. It is essential to recognize the difference between the two. Think of a *goal* as something external that somebody else suggested or imposed. (This is not necessarily good or bad, because external goals, if properly aligned, can help us achieve our inner goal, which is our purpose in life.) A *purpose*, on the other hand, is something that comes from within; it has been created or found by oneself. A purpose in what you do may not coincide with your present company's mission, but it also does not necessarily need to be a transcendental one. Your purpose could be a high and noble cause, such as saving lives, finding a cure for a rare disease, creating something the world has never seen before, educating at-risk kids, solving an environmental conundrum, creating quality objects that stimulate positive feelings in consumers, developing an environment-friendly mind-set in your community, or elevating moods and spirits by producing a piece of art or writing songs. Your purpose also could represent less far-fetched aspirations (and those closer to our business world), such as improving working relationships in your organization, turning the challenges of leadership into opportunities for personal growth, developing a culture that brings out the best in your people, or mentoring up-and-coming leaders.

Think of purpose as something that you find pleasure in pursuing and that you would like to be remembered for—your legacy (the question Richard was not able to answer). A purpose provides direction. It is the reason I get up every morning, and it will help me weather some difficult times. It is the caffeine (with no side effects!) that Richard needed to help him become more resilient to external adversities (criticism from his boss), and it might have prevented him from making such an abrupt decision (resigning). Richard could not bear an insignificant *how* because he had not yet found a *why* for his existence.

In my personal case, and after a long process of self-discovery, I found that my purpose is to help elevate the level of self-awareness in the people who work with me (and I really hope that this book can help you do the same). It is something that I find pleasure in and has not been externally imposed on me. As a business leader, I have many goals to achieve (many of which are contained in the performance-management reports I receive from my stakeholders). I am deeply convinced that my ultimate goal, my purpose in life, will help me and my group become more effective so that, hopefully, we can more easily reach the goals that my company's stakeholders set.

Purpose—The First P of the Self-Awareness Ring

Purpose	The first step toward a higher level of self-consciousness is discovering what our inner purpose is. We must ask ourselves honest questions about what really drives us and what brings significance to

our lives, which by definition needs to go beyond material success or any of the above-mentioned mechanistic motives (popularity, status, money, or power). It is an individual work that will need effort and time. It revolves around knowing oneself on a deeper level. It will vary from person to person. Generally speaking, a high level of self-consciousness produces the following effects on the individual:

- It fosters full engagement in activities. It is the striving to find a meaning in one's life—the primary, most powerful motivating and driving force in humans.

  Richard had a tough time seeking motivation in what he did; the utter absence of an inner purpose deprived him of the possibility to make the daily routines at work become something valuable. In a totally opposite case, I learned from a person doing a supposedly menial job—a cleaning lady at a hospital—how highly engaged one can be while doing routine tasks. She told me that the purpose of her job was to keep people healthy and that the better she performed her task, the lower the possibility was that diseases would spread, which brought her a lot of satisfaction and motivated her to do her best every single day.

- It allows a person to create a fuller contribution by using his or her personal strengths. We are born with certain talents that can be developed further in our lives. Often you will find your inner purpose by paying more attention to what you are good at. We will be able to make a more robust contribution if we play on our strengths. The trick here is to understand better what we really like and enjoy, what comes naturally to us, and what makes us happy.

  Peter was a medical rep, who was promoted to sales manager due to his excellent results, for a major multinational company. Still, after a few months, he decided to go back to his previous position.

He loved interacting with physicians and found pleasure in providing them with information that allowed them to make better prescription decisions, even if they sometimes were at the expense of the product line he was carrying. Still, the passion and honesty with which he conducted himself usually convinced doctors to opt for Peter's product brands every time they had a choice.

• It allows you to focus on something larger than your own self. As previously mentioned, a purpose is something that you would like to be remembered for and that transcends yourself.

Brad was honored with a lifetime-achievement award at his company's year-end party. His colleagues selected him not on the basis of his unit results for the previous twenty-five years but on the changes he made to his subordinates' lives. He was a highly respected mentor who created such a high level of trust within the teams he led that most team members were eager to open themselves up and expose their areas of developmental weakness. Few people could remember what the sales turnover growth rates were (which, by the way, were among the top rates in the company). Several people expressed their deep gratitude for how much they had learned from Brad, particularly on a personal level. We always remember people, like our schoolteachers, who take the time to listen to us actively and to care for our personal growth selflessly.

Starting the quest for your purpose in life will, first and foremost, contribute to your personal enrichment and impact your whole self—physically, emotionally, psychologically, and spiritually. It will contribute to your personal growth, and one of the consequences will be a higher level of effectiveness in your leadership skills. The higher your level of consciousness, the easier this task will become. A deep and transcendent purpose will also energize all of your interdependent stakeholders, including your employees, your customers, and the communities in which your company interacts.

There are many ways to practice the skill to delve into your own self. My personal advice is to sample as many ways as you can and then stick with the one that best suits your present needs. (It will most certainly vary according to the phase you are going through, and some techniques will prove more or less effective with time.)

Here are some examples of ways to develop your level of self-awareness and, consequently, your ability to find your purpose in life:

- **Seeking counseling or therapy**—I highly recommend hiring a licensed psychologist, not a trained life coach, because a coach often addresses only the symptoms, not the causes, of behavioral change.
- **Writing a personal diary**—This will work, provided you have the discipline and the objectivity to record your daily personal experiences in an unbiased and nonjudgmental way.
- **Attending self-development workshops**—The more specific the topic, the better, such as active listening skills, resilience, influencing with authority, development of empathy skills, participative leadership, and diversity.
- **Taking personality tests**—Consider those that provide 360-degree feedback, like the Inner Theater Inventory® by Manfred Kets de Vries and the Myers–Briggs Type Indicator® personality inventory.
- **Brainstorming exercises**—They can reveal your hidden/dormant talents when you ask yourself the following questions:
  o What world issues disturb you the most and are the ones you could make the biggest impact on?
  o When have you been most passionate and enthusiastic about a specific task?
  o When have you found the most pleasure in your work?
  o What would you take a strong stand for, regardless of other people's opinions?
  o What type of activities do you gravitate toward outside of work that you feel respected for?

- **Practicing yoga and meditation**—Those who systematically pursue this combination cite that it is an effective stress reliever that builds strength and stability, as well as mental clarity and discipline.
- **Reading about sociology, psychology, or philosophy matters from the authors you like the most**—There are many ways to approach these seemingly obscure fields, and one of them is to read books that reference the classics or combine deep psychology with humor. My favorite books are the three that combine famous rabbi and psychiatrist Abraham Twerski's patients' life stories with the humor of the *Peanuts* cartoons, titled *When Do the Good Things Start?, A Therapist Looks at Life's Ups and Downs* and *With a Bit of Help from Charlie Brown and His Friends.*[3]
- **Reading biographies or other types of books about people you admire**—Viktor Frankl, the author of *Man's Search for Meaning*, said that the pedagogical path to learn to find meaning in our lives is to study those who have found a meaning in theirs.
- **Doing visualization exercises**
  - o Close your eyes and picture yourself at your own funeral and surrounded by your loved ones. Try, without passing any judgment, to see and hear what your family and friends say about you. What are the things they remember most or the most vivid shared experiences? Most importantly, what have been the effects of your own actions on them? What was your impact on their lives? In summary, what is your legacy?
  - o Picture yourself surrounded by unspoiled nature, in a place you would love to be. Dwell on this sensation of pure pleasure for a few minutes until these feelings are imprinted on your mind. Then scan the major activities you have done in the past years until you find the ones that provoke the same kind of feeling. Your purpose in

life should be built around those areas that trigger these positive sensations.

o   Ask yourself what you would do if you happened to know that this would be the last year of your life. Stop for a while to reflect on what came to your mind, and write it down. Now ask yourself the same question, but instead assume you have just one month of life. Continue with this routine until you reach the minimum time span (say, five minutes). Pause for a while, and afterward, browse through the list of things you wrote until you find a common pattern.

o   On a more positive note, picture yourself at the young age of eighteen. Knowing what you know now, what kind of advice would you give to that confused boy or girl?

As Age of Aquarius as it may sound, visualization is pretty much based on deep philosophical concepts. (Actually, the phrase "Age of Aquarius" comes from a statement in Plato's dialogues about it being the place where humanity will reach once reason, logic, and harmony have freed our minds and brought us to utopia, or a better world.)

Finding your purpose entails going back to your roots with the help of different methods that will enable you to have a better insight into your own self. It involves deeply questioning what you do and why is it that you are here on this earth. Of course the journey is not easy, but it is well worth trying. As the famous Greek philosopher Socrates said, "The unexamined life is not worth living."[4]

Do not get discouraged if your inner purpose does not come out immediately or changes frequently. You do not need to spend your whole life looking for the meaning of life; you just need to be true to yourself and to your own emotions and senses. By diving into a deeper level of consciousness, by knowing yourself better, you will be building your own purpose *while* you live. As Viktor Frankl said, "What matters, therefore, is not the meaning of life in general but rather the specific meaning of a person's life at a given moment."

A purpose in life will become the anchor that will allow you to weather the many storms you will experience. And one of the consequences of discovering your purpose is that you will move away from a constant planning state of mind into a deeper immersion in the *present* moment. It will cause you to shift your attention from your career (future) to your job (present). This ability to focus on the *present* constitutes the second P of our self-awareness ring, which is what the next chapter is about.

Chapter Three

JOB OR CAREER?

There is no future
There is no past
I live this moment
As my last
There's only us
There's only this
Forget regret
Or life is yours to miss
No other road
No other way
No day but today
—Jonathan Larson, "Another Day" (from *Rent*)

Paige did not think twice; she responded rapidly when posed with a question about where she saw herself in five years' time during her last job interview. She was not eager to understand what she would actually do if she got hired. All she knew was that by joining this world-class consumer-goods company, she would be able to make her résumé much more appealing for future employers; she would be able to aspire to better jobs in a short period of time. When the interviewer started to elaborate on the different aspects of the position, Paige just was not there; all that mattered was to get a foot into that company's door. She already had a prestigious education, and now it was time to work for companies with prestigious names in her professional life. The experienced interviewer decided to offer Paige the job, even though he clearly understood Paige's intentions and the fact that she would not stay there for very long. (She ended up staying there for less than a year.) But hey, hiring an MBA from Harvard was a way for the interviewer to be appreciated by his own boss, and the more Ivy-League hires he could get, the faster his own career would grow.

Mark wanted to have an in-depth discussion about his career plan with his boss, even though it had been only three months since he had joined the company. He wanted to understand clearly what it would take to be assigned to the emerging-markets area. He knew that, at this particular consulting firm, if he stayed in the area of mature markets, it would take at least five years to become a senior partner, but if he worked in this other, faster developing area of business (where senior-management attention seemed to be), chances were that he could get to the same position of senior partner in just three years. Granted, working in emerging markets meant traveling at least two hundred days per year and doing a job that was not very appealing to him. The topic of Mark's graduate thesis and his interest was investigating mature-market dynamics and ways of turning business around; he had loved studying those issues when he was at the university. But the final prize of a faster-moving career was worth abandoning his passion. Moreover, all that traveling would surely make a dent in his present relationship, but he figured business is business, and three years go by very quickly when one is just thirty years old. His fiancée would understand. Additionally, as a senior partner, he would be able to build an optimal network that surely would help him build his own business down the road. His plan was to open his own consulting firm before turning forty.

Neither Paige nor Mark was particularly interested in the content of their jobs or even in how much money they would make. Their goal was just to obtain a fast career, regardless of what it would take. In Paige's case, the intent was to hop from one big company to another, as if they were stepping stones in the race toward a bright and happy future. She would just have to pretend that she would do anything for the company that hired her, even though she would start looking for a better job the minute she got in; it was a question of collecting bigger and bigger names on her résumé to aspire to better and better jobs in the future. In company jargon, she would be considered a highflier, an extremely talented and ambitious person who is hard to retain. Many consulting firms and large consumer-goods companies are used to playing this same game, trading the company reputation with these young candidates in exchange for extra work (and low pay). They know that some people are willing to sacrifice a balance of work life and private life (those employees who are willing to go the extra mile) if they can have a prestigious name on their résumés to help them get in with even better companies.

Mark's case was a little less extreme. He was passionate about what he did, but he was willing to put those passions aside for a while, sacrificing the present for an imagined better future. It is not uncommon to come across people who do not like what they presently do, and many times they even have the opportunity to follow their hearts if they want to. They stay in their unsatisfying jobs because they have the illusion that they are building their future and that, down the road, the time will come when they will be able to do what they like.

Rarely did it occur to either Paige or Mark whether they would actually enjoy what they were supposed to do or not or whether the jobs would help them realize their own passions or not. It was as if they were not working on a *job* but purely on a *career*...they were flat out avoiding the present by living in the future. But the future is just a construction we create in our minds, not an actual entity; there is no certainty that that construction will ever materialize. This is not only because there is no certainty we will be alive but also because experience tells us that what we dream or plan for rarely happens. Paige and Mark were wasting away their lives by becoming distracted with the illusion of creating or controlling their futures. They were avoiding the present. They were seriously lacking *the consciousness of the present moment.*

Presence—The Second P of the Self-Awareness Ring

Purpose
Presence

The Dalai Lama said that what surprised him most of humankind was that "man is so anxious about the future that he does not enjoy the present, the result being that he does not live in the present or the future; he lives as if he is never going to die, and then dies having never really lived." And many others have talked extensively about the joy of living in the present and the futility of staying in the past or looking only to the future, consequently disregarding the only thing we have: *the present moment.* Tons of books have been written about this human flaw of living something that is not real. Still, it seems that we have learned little despite the fact that we are constantly being reminded of this very basic concept. We are told over and over again, "Carpe diem," seize the moment. Yes, we can, and need to, use the past as a learning experience, and we also need to be prepared for what the future will bring. The point here is to avoid getting attached to either the past or the future if we want to avoid one of the frequent causes of our suffering. Hindu prince Siddhartha Gautama, the founder of Buddhism, said, "Do not dwell in the past; do not dream of the future. Concentrate the mind on the present moment."[1] But it seems to take more than one Buddha or more than two thousand years of Western civilization to overcome this tendency. We do not need to delve into religion to acknowledge this fact. Much more recently, Eckhart Tolle, in his book *The Power of Now,*[2] stated that our mode of consciousness can be transformed and that the way to become free of the egotistical mind is to become deeply conscious of this present moment, or, as he often calls it, "the Now." To be present is to become reconnected not only with our dissociated self but also to be able to connect with others in a much deeper way. Granted, many times the present does not look that pleasant, and by living in the future, we may think we can evade the difficulties and obstacles that life places in our way. But avoiding the present makes us suffer even more; we will eventually be forced to accept what reality puts in front of us, regardless of what we do. By attempting to live in the future, all that we do is bring the future to the present. *The future is now.* Eckhart Tolle goes beyond this notion of living in the present moment and speaks of surrendering to the flow of life and accepting the present moment unconditionally and without reservation. There are many examples that are even closer to our daily lives. The lyrics from the musical *Rent* at the beginning of this chapter emphasize the need to grasp the present moment if you do not want to miss what life is all about because, after all, *life is what actually happens while you are busy making plans.*[3] And even closer, who has never heard from their grandparents that we need to seize the moment, to enjoy it at its fullest, because that is all we eventually have?

Focusing our attention on the present moment influences many aspects of our lives and significantly impacts our own behavior and the people we manage.

Planning vs. Being Prepared for the Future

Many company executives live in the future by constructing extremely elaborate long-term business and career plans. On the business side, it is funny to note that even though these ten-year projections are being reviewed every single year—often with dramatic changes—few people question the utility (or futility) of a long-term plan. Likewise, rarely have I met a person whose actual career path matched the one he or she had planned in advance. We pretend to act as if the future will be an outcome of our projections.

I am absolutely not intending to disregard the importance of the future in our lives. As responsible business leaders, we all need to *be prepared* for what the future will bring. (We will always need our strategic-planning departments). Living in the present does not imply that we do not care about what the future will bring. It is our job to do our utmost to get our companies in the best possible shape to weather problems and tap into opportunities the future will bring. It is our duty to work on forecasts, run future scenarios, and develop strategies for various potential outcomes. Forecasts help us to *be prepared* for what the future will eventually bring. We don't know the future, and we will not know it until it's no longer the future. The illusion is to assume that we can *plan* our future—that it is an eventual certainty if we take the right steps and behave in a certain way. We all laugh when we hear young people say that they will get married by a certain age, have a certain number of kids, etc., but we take it seriously in our professional lives when we discuss our career plan with our bosses. That is why cases like Mark's or Paige's do not seem to be that uncommon in our companies. The effect of this linear thinking, this constant planning mentality, will produce the opposite of what we want to achieve. Once the future arrives, and most probably contradicts what we had planned to happen, we are caught by surprise ("How come this happened?") and are unprepared to face the new reality.

I believe a healthier way to deal with uncertainty is to consider different scenarios and work diligently to figure out what the result will be if a certain scenario comes true. Some analysts do work on optimistic, realistic, and pessimistic scenarios, but several times they superficially address the first and last and focus only on the so-called realistic one because that is the one they assume will happen. If, on the other hand, we honestly accept the *tyranny of contingency*—the element of uncertainty that rules all events in life—we will work much harder to train our people and to develop those skills that prepare us for any future. The skills include the following:

- **Resilience** is the ability to adapt and bounce back when things do not go as originally planned. We may deem failures what, many times, are just facts of life—the fact that the future sometimes does not materialize as we want it to. It is, therefore, key to make sure we focus our energies on things we can control and view failures as opportunities to learn from and grow, not as paralyzing events. There are many ways to develop our capacity for resilience (as well as that of our working teams), which is characterized by positive thinking and self-confidence. Furthermore, the clearer your personal and work goals are, the stronger your level of commitment will be to succeed, despite any temporary setbacks you may face.

- **Cognitive restructuring** is the ability to manage distorted thoughts. We are all going to fall and fail sometimes, but we need to do it with awareness—with equanimity. We cannot control events, but we can choose *how* we respond to them. Cognitive restructuring teaches us to maintain perspective, see the effects of unplanned events as temporary rather than permanent, and avoid overreacting or letting setbacks impact other unrelated areas of our lives. There are many approaches to developing this skill, and it is highly advisable to do it first with the help of an organizational psychologist. For further understanding of this concept, I strongly recommend the book *Mind Over Mood* by Drs. Dennis Greenberger and Christine Padesky.
- **Stress management** is the ability to react to stress in a positive manner and take control of the situation, rather than allowing the stress to remain the prominent focus. Because we have the illusion that we can control everything, including the future, we can react to a challenging or unexpected situation by becoming frazzled or feeling overwhelmed or distraught. As previously mentioned, we cannot control the external events, but we do have full command of how we respond to them. By controlling our reactions in a positive manner, we can alleviate the stress and actually make it work in our favor. There are many tips out there on how to alleviate stress, and most of them consider not only your mind but also your body. The better you take care of both of them, the more effective you will become at coping with life's challenges and overcoming setbacks.

Being Present and Its Effects on Productivity

Many of us will try to build our own future and candidly assume that this will be possible; we will sacrifice the present for a better future. (We will invest in our future.) Nevertheless, it seems that encouraging that kind of behavior in our organizations may not be the most effective way of running a business and actually may have a deleterious effect. If, as a company employee, I am focused only on my future career, will I dedicate all of my efforts to solving the everyday issues my company is facing? Or will I otherwise (even subconsciously) prioritize my battles based on the effect a positive outcome of the selected ones will have on my career? If I prioritize my career (future) over my job (present), it is quite likely that my level of connectedness to the people I interact with in the office will not reach a profound level because those people just happened to be there for a short period of time on the road to my upward career. My boss, my colleagues, the company I work for, and the job I do are simply means that will allow me to conquer my ultimate goal: moving up the corporate ladder.

Additionally, as stated earlier, when people are obsessed with their *future*, it is likely that their *present* gets somewhat neglected, thus impacting the quality of their work. Those people are the ones who make impressive and exciting presentations to senior management and are all fired up in front of their bosses, but they immediately succumb once the lights are off. What can be more depressing than pursuing something unattainable (the future) at the expense of sacrificing the passion of enjoying the only thing that is real (*the present moment*)? How often have you seen real joy in those highfliers/achievers? Yes, I am sure they are emptily proclaiming to everybody that they are having fun—and they are being about as convincing as a politician during a campaign. Even if they are actually having fun from time to time, is that enough? Are they really enjoying the ride?

Without passing any judgment on either Mark or Paige, my experience tells me that these corporate climbers are rarely happy. How can they experience the joy of the present if all they are focused on is their future, which, by definition, will never arrive? This amounts to an increasing sense of frustration and anger. Heedless upward mobility, for all the luxuries it affords, looks pretty grim.

The Difference between Fun and Pleasure

Many times I hear from business leaders that they are having fun in their jobs. There is the *fun* part, when employees are urged to have fun, during many company workshops. We are all supposed to look happy, and those who do not are frowned upon. Politicians always seem to be having lots of fun, with huge smiles on their faces at every photo opportunity. Assuming that, even from time to time, one experiences fun in what he or she does, this cannot be an indicator of self-realization. There is a big difference between having fun and feeling pleasure. Fun provides amusement and enjoyment through playful, often boisterous activity that is externally induced, often for a short duration. We cannot feel fun; we can just do fun things, and, therefore, we need to depend on external factors. Moreover, when these fun moments subside, a feeling of emptiness remains...The various achievements at work (promotions, praise from bosses, attainment of goals, etc.) do not seem to be enough to grant peace of mind. On the other hand, living in the present, pursuing excellence in what we actually do—regardless of the effect this will have in our careers—will allow us to feel pleasure and an internal condition of the mind that needs no external inducement: I am content with what I do in the present moment, and I do not need my boss to motivate me, to give me constant positive feedback, or to reward me with a pat on the back or with a promotion. The *attainment of excellence* is its own reward. As a leader, I will become more independent of criticism, more secure in my own strengths.

How Present Are You?

We are always online, constantly connected through social media with our friends, always planning our next steps. On the other hand, despite this supposedly high level of connectivity, it is common to forget the small indicators that are signals of our actual *disconnection* with reality. For example, we take a shower and shampoo twice because we forget we did it the first time. We forget what we just had for lunch. Or the minute we hang up the phone with a friend, we forget what we talked about. We miss life because we are just not involved with what is happening to us and to our surroundings. And at work, we see similar signals of disconnection with the present. A quick personal exercise you can do to measure your level of consciousness in the present moment is to answer the following statements honestly with "yes" or "no":

- I update my CV more than twice a year.
- My boss should motivate me more.
- I do not want to stay in the same position for more than one year.
- In some years, I will be able to run my own business.
- I have always worked for big companies.
- I stay in touch with headhunters as often as I can.
- Networking is key for my career and prevails over friendship at work.
- I am willing to sacrifice some years doing what I do not like if that means achieving my career plan more quickly.
- I firmly believe in career plans.
- I am in control of my own future.

It is quite likely that the more you answer *yes* to the above statements, the less focused on the present you may be and the less connected you are with yourself and with the people and things surrounding you. It is hard to be in deep touch with the present if your mind is focused on your future career moves!

Consequently, leading with consciousness requires that we find our purpose in life—something we like and that we would like to be remembered for. As a second step, it requires that we focus on what we have (the present) instead of being distracted by an illusion of something we cannot act on anymore (the past) or control (the future); we need to have a quiet mind that lives in the moment and is disturbed by neither the past nor the future. The higher *your* level of presence, the greater the possibility of enjoying what you do (feeling pleasure) and the greater the likelihood that your productivity will increase, the closer your bonds will be with the people surrounding you, and the more concerned you will become with their personal growth as individuals. You will develop the leadership competence of *authority care*—what you do and say will influence others. Your concern with the present will make your actions selfless, and you will not fear adversity.

This is, of course, a lifelong quest for personal growth, and there are many steps you need to take to become a conscious leader (and a better person). You will need to understand yourself on a deeper level and aim to achieve a healthy internal balance between your level of self-awareness and your level of self-confidence, which will result in a positive self-image. That is the subject of the next chapter.

Chapter Four

SELF-AWARENESS AND SELF-CONFIDENCE

When I was younger, so much younger than today,
I never needed anybody's help in any way,
But now these days are gone, and I'm not so self-assured,
Now I find I've changed my mind; I've opened up the doors.
Help me if you can, I'm feeling down,
And I do appreciate you being around,
Help me get my feet back on the ground,
Won't you please, please help me?
—The Beatles, "Help!"

Jack graduated with honors from MIT and straight afterward decided to accept a job as an analyst reporting directly to the CEO of a multinational conglomerate. In his job, Jack had the opportunity to interact face to face with members of the executive committee, which helped him to understand better how the company operated from the top of the pyramid. This position fit well with Jack's aspiration of becoming a managing director at one of the company's subsidiaries within a short period of time. Even though he was just turning twenty-six, Jack knew he could make it; after all, during his stay at MIT, he was ranked among the top 5 percent and had achieved outstanding ratings in strategic planning and general management.

After one year of working at this new company, during Jack's yearly performance assessment, the CEO pointed out to Jack some of the areas he would have to work on if he wanted to become a managing director.

For instance, Jack needed to build some experience in the field, where he would be confronted with real people problems. Jack had strong analytical skills, but he needed some experience making the transition from theory to practice. He was good at building complex scenarios and coming up with innovative solutions, but he needed to prove that he could make things happen through the people he would lead. That is why the CEO decided to offer him a position as sales director leading a group of one hundred sales representatives and reporting to one of the members of the CEO's executive team. Jack could not believe his ears; this meant an actual demotion (or at least that is how Jack interpreted the fact that his future boss would be one of his former peers on the executive committee team). Jack was deeply convinced it should have been the other way around; he should be replacing any one of the members of the executive team instead of becoming one of their subordinates. After all, he thought, he was the only one who held an MBA from a top-notch university, while all these little people sitting on the executive committee came from much less prestigious institutions. How on earth could he report to somebody he could not look up to and, therefore, had nothing to learn from? The discussion between Jack and his CEO evolved into a heated argument; Jack reacted emotionally and even showed disrespect toward his boss. In his mind, he could not conceive why this stupid CEO could not see all the value Jack was bringing to the company. Jack was sure he possessed an IQ that was much higher than any other executive in that company (and for that matter, much higher than that of this mentally challenged CEO). He was almost sure that these people were just hiding behind their field experience because they had limited academic records and were afraid of his innovative ideas and superb analytical skills.

The CEO was stunned at Jack's almost hysterical and childish emotional reaction. He brought up Jack's low level of emotional intelligence; he also tried to show how this new job could help Jack improve this personality weakness of his. Jack snorted his contempt with a smug grin on his face, thinking these people were making a lame excuse to terminate him. In fact, Jack thought, even the CEO was not that bright and most probably was feeling envious of Jack's outstanding academic record. Jack was sure he would promptly find other companies with wiser men who would be able to appreciate his value proposition. He decided to present his resignation.

As absurd as this case may seem (which, by the way, was a real-life situation I personally experienced), it is unfortunately not that uncommon in our business world. Furthermore, this low level of self-awareness can be seen all the way up to the top of the organizational pyramid. In many incidences, even much more experienced executives may not seem to have an accurate picture of their strengths and weaknesses. One of the reasons is that, unfortunately, people often place little emphasis on their ability to understand themselves. For instance, one of the worldwide leading business institutions, the Center for Creative Leadership, asked pharmaceutical executives about the most critical competencies for success in their organizations. When asked to rank the sixteen top competencies according to how important each was for success, the following list of the top eight and bottom eight competencies resulted.

Top Eight Leadership Competencies:

- Leading employees
- Strategic perspective
- Decisiveness
- Change management
- Composure
- Building collaborative relationships
- Participative management
- Taking initiative

Bottom Eight Leadership Competencies:

- Being a quick study
- Self-awareness
- Confronting problem employees
- Balance between personal and work life

- Compassion and sensitivity
- Respect for differences
- Career management
- Putting people at ease

The ability to lead employees was rated as the most important quality needed for effective leadership, topping the list for 90 percent of the pharmaceutical executives who provided performance data on leaders in their organizations. The top eight competencies shown above were each endorsed by the majority of respondents who worked in the pharmaceutical sector. As you can see, the competency of self-awareness was ranked among the bottom eight. The question is, how can someone lead an organization effectively if he or she is not able to lead him or herself first? How can someone know their employees if they do not first have a deep understanding of themselves, their strengths and weaknesses, their behaviors, and how they impact their teams?

Positive Self-Image—the Third P of Self-Awareness

Purpose
Presence
Positive self-image

Assertiveness is one of the required competencies of any effective leader. It is a necessary condition to believe in yourself if you want others to believe in you. How can you ever lead anybody if you do not portray a strong level of self-confidence?

Rarely in my professional life have I ever encountered self-confidence issues with senior managers or executives. One does not make it to the top level of a multibillion-dollar corporation unless he or she possesses a strong belief in his or her abilities—a *positive self-image*. A big part of this comes from us, from the way we were born and brought up; it is part of our genes and personality. But it is also built from the experiences and knowledge we have gained over time in our professional lives. Self-confidence shows how prepared you are to face challenges; it is all about knowing what you want and about believing with all your heart that you will be able to achieve your goals.

It is important to note that believing in yourself, believing in your ideas, and standing up for them even against adversity does not mean that you are better than any of your colleagues or that your ideas are the best ones. Unfortunately, many times we struggle to discern between confidence and competence, which can then result into the election of self-centered and narcissistic individuals as leaders, even though arrogance and overconfidence are inversely related to leadership skills. And this is the importance of possessing a good level of *self-awareness*—a good leader needs to have a healthy balance between the two, and experience tells us that the second part of the equation is the one that we, as leaders, have more trouble dealing with. It is also where *our level of consciousness is lower*. Knowing what your areas of developmental weakness are and being able to accept your weaknesses as much as you accept your strengths are key elements of our success as leaders, and most importantly, of our happiness as human beings.

Emotional Maturity

Emotional intelligence, EQ, is a behavioral model that gained popularity around 1995 with Daniel Goleman's first book on this subject.[1] The EQ concept argues that IQ (intelligence quotient), or conventional intelligence, is too narrow and that there are wider areas of emotional intelligence that dictate and enable how successful we can become. Success, therefore, requires more than a high IQ, which has tended to be the traditional measure of intelligence, and it is essential not to ignore the role behavioral and character elements play. EQ embraces understanding yourself, your intentions, others, and their feelings. It is the ability to understand the impact your behavior can have on others. We have all met people who are academically brilliant (Jack is one example), yet they are socially and interpersonally inept so that, despite possessing a high IQ, success does not automatically follow. (I believe you may find some examples at class reunions, where you realize that some former outstanding colleagues of yours are working in miserable jobs.)

Before this concept of EQ came out in the business field, psychologists (and for that matter, our own parents!) named this personality trait *emotional maturity*. It's the ability to be conscious of your intentions, feelings, strengths, and flaws; the ability to understand what the effect of your actions have on the others; and, most importantly, the ability to imagine yourself in somebody else's shoes.

For many years, business leaders started to pay attention to these behaviors, and manager performance started to be measured on this subjective aspect, on top of the usual business metrics. For instance, despite achieving sound, short-term financial results or being a subject-matter expert, a narcissistic leader in an organization can be a ticking bomb (and this, unfortunately, is not that uncommon). A narcissistic leader will not only have an unfair balance between his or her level of self-confidence and self-awareness, but even his or her high level of self-confidence may not be real. The person may be hiding inner feelings of inadequacy by conveying a false sense of high self-esteem and assertiveness but secretly longing for constant recognition. Frequently, a troubled childhood denies these insecure people the positive reinforcement any person needs to develop in a healthy way. When these people receive any minor criticism, they take it personally, perceive it as an attack, and repel it aggressively. Unfortunately, Jack is not such a rare example of this character flaw that pervades our organizations. Many Jacks coming from prestigious academic institutions have created serious damage within organizations that take a long time to heal; no wonder these kind of personalities very rarely stay in the same company a long time. They may look extremely convincing during a job interview, and their outstanding academic record may divert the attention of the interviewer from the behaviors he or she has to assess accurately to determine if the individual possesses a healthy balance between confidence and awareness. As logical as this may sound, very often EQ is neglected when interviewing candidates for specialist jobs. We tend to focus our attention on the academic and job-experience qualifications of the candidate and disregard the social aspects. Additionally, in an effort to avoid any risk of being sued for discrimination, we skip any question that can appear to be personal and not professional, with the illusion that we can dissect a person into different stagnant compartments. We hold the false hope that the person will bring only his or her sensing and thinking side to the office and leave his or her emotions and intuition at home. (In Part Three of this book, I discuss the importance of looking at employees in a holistic and not a mechanistic way.)

Embrace Your Weaknesses

A couple thousand years ago, the Greeks already had a clear concept of emotional maturity. Aristotle said that knowing and understanding oneself was the key to true knowledge; Socrates's life principle was to "know thyself." In fact, Socrates was convinced that true knowledge and moral virtues were inscribed within the soul of each individual; learning was then just cultivating the soul, the self, and making one's implicit understanding of truth explicit.

It is hard to find a school of thought that does not perceive the self as the starting point of the perception of reality and of others. As a leader, I will never be able to develop people if I do not know myself in depth and the impact my behaviors and actions have on others. Developing and reinforcing this skill is a lifelong task. The deeper the insight we have into ourselves, the higher our *level of consciousness* will be and the better we will be able to make a positive impact on others. The stronger the insight of our strengths and weaknesses, the better leaders and persons we will become.

It is important to note that the focus of our attention is placed on the awareness of our weaknesses and not on the effort it will take to improve or eliminate them. We will be able to lean on our strengths to manage around our weaknesses, but very rarely will we be able to improve character traits and flaws that may come all the way from our childhood, from the way in which we were brought up, and from the early experiences that have almost permanently modified our psyches. Through psychotherapy, we can examine the areas where we feel more vulnerable and become more aware of our limitations, but trying to eliminate them may be a frustrating uphill battle. As the famous prayer goes, "God, grant me the serenity to accept the things I cannot change, courage to change the things I can, and wisdom to know the difference."[2]

We may be able to recognize our strengths somewhat (even though this ability is also highly overrated), but it takes a greater effort to accept what we cannot do or become, even if we want to. Contrary to common sense, we will be able to *increase* our self-confidence by actually *acknowledging our weaknesses*. The more we know about our shortcomings and the more we publicly show this awareness, the stronger our level of self-confidence will be. We have to expose our flaws if we intend to build stronger teams that will help us circumnavigate those areas where our expertise is limited. Contrary to the know-it-all leader, we will be *self-aware leaders* who will look for people who can compensate for what we lack. Our organizations will benefit more from leaders who take responsibility for what they don't know than they will from leaders who pretend to know it all. This may sound counterintuitive in our modern society, in which competition gets tougher and harsher. In fact, many of us in leading positions operate on the illusion that we need to appear as though we know everything all the time or else people will question our abilities, our knowledge, and ultimately our effectiveness as leaders. We may be perceived as old-fashioned, not keeping up with the fast pace of life, and, therefore, replaceable, but, actually, the opposite is true. Regardless of your level of self-awareness, your team will very well see where your shortcomings are, and the worst thing you can do is hide your flaws. Everyone sees them, and by attempting to conceal them, all you will do is project a perception of a lack of integrity. Self-awareness about your strengths and weaknesses will earn you the trust of others and increase your level of credibility, and this will increase your leadership effectiveness. The higher the insight into ourselves, the higher the level of consciousness.

SWOT Analysis

A practical way to increase your level of consciousness about your own strengths and weaknesses is through an anonymous 360-degree feedback tool. I highly recommend that you go beyond the web-based, multiple-choice tools and hire a trained professional to interview each one of the respondents confidentially to obtain better qualitative insights into their feedback. You can do the same for each one of your team members so that you can acquire a list of the weaknesses and strengths of the people you lead. Based on that information, you can all then conduct a SWOT (Strengths, Weaknesses, Opportunities, and Threats) analysis very much like you do when you need to evaluate a project or business venture. It is like doing strategic planning, whereby the objective is not solving a business matter but improving your leadership skills. The *internal* strengths and weaknesses are the ones your group identifies in you, while the *external* opportunities and threats are the strengths and weaknesses your team members possess. This tool will allow you to scan the working environment objectively and, together with your group, find ways to manage around your weaknesses by tapping into the opportunities your teammates present. Funny as this may sound to our analytical minds, this can be the first step toward developing much more honest communication among your team members. (If you find this too extreme, first do this exercise with your family and see how it goes!)

The Three Ps of the Self-Awareness Ring

We have discussed the need to find or create a *purpose* in our lives, to focus our attention on the *present* moment, and to work on a *positive self-image,* striking a healthy balance between self-awareness and self-confidence. These three elements constitute the starting point of our process of self-discovery and immersion into a deeper *level of consciousness*, which will help us integrate our dissociated selves. First, we must start working on our internal ring of self-awareness before we even attempt to help our employees, because the higher our own level of consciousness, the higher the level of consciousness of our working teams. The stronger the inner ring, the more solid the foundation of the outer rings—people and community—will become. We need to start by integrating ourselves before we can help our team members integrate among themselves and integrate the team within the community.

PART THREE

THE TEAM-AWARENESS RING

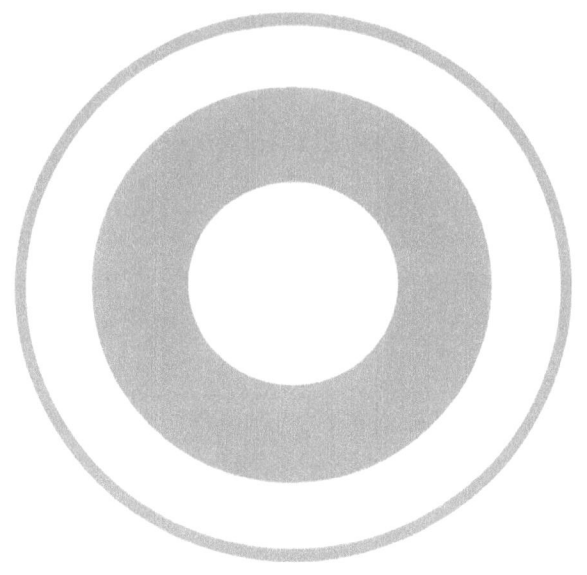

Chapter Five

TEAM AWARENESS

Give 'em the old razzle-dazzle
Razzle dazzle 'em
Give 'em an act with lots of flash in it
And the reaction will be passionate
Give 'em the old hocus-pocus
Bead and feather 'em
How can they see with sequins in their eyes?
What if your hinges all are rusting?
What if, in fact, you're just disgusting?
Razzle dazzle 'em
And they'll never catch wise!
—"Razzle Dazzle," *Chicago, the Musical*

First Things First

Susan took over the West Coast area of a logistics company. Her management team consisted of ten professionals who were having several issues with their former boss. Susan was told that her managers were ten isolated but clever minds who were not willing to work together; each one would deliver on what he or she would be asked to do, provided it did not involve a high level of interaction with the other team members. They all were reserved people and jealous of what their counterparts would accomplish. Staff meetings were extremely boring, and the only interaction was between Susan and each of the team members separately; they would never comment on their colleagues' work and were extremely reluctant to share best practices or even pay attention when a team member would present ideas. Each would defend his or her own territory, and nobody would ever dare to try a different approach. This was the way things were done in the past, and results showed that there was no need to change working processes.

Susan thought much differently. She was coming from a long process of self-discovery with the help of an organizational psychologist and was convinced that having an integrated team would help each member raise his or her level of awareness and ultimately increase the overall team's effectiveness. Susan's purpose was to help elevate the level of awareness of her team members and connect each one of them first with themselves and then with a higher cause in their lives. She decided to hire her psychologist and have him work with her team members. This person would surely not be welcome with open arms by her group, but because it was Susan's idea, they would at least have to tolerate him. After a few sessions, the team members asked Susan to discontinue the coaching sessions. They all felt that the process did not add any professional value and that the psychologist was getting into personal matters instead of just focusing on professional ones. They said they would prefer to have a coach who would help them be more effective at making presentations, increase the effectiveness of their meetings, learn tips on facilitative leadership, etc. Susan, afraid of the possibility of being sued by anyone claiming interference in private matters, fired the guy and focused on what the team requested. After two years, productivity in Susan's area was lagging behind, and communication among team members was still an issue.

What went wrong? It seems that Susan started her own trip toward a higher level of consciousness, but she was having difficulty convincing her team to do the same.

My first advice to her would be that she should focus on the three Ps of the inner circle (find a clearly defined *purpose*, focus on the *present* moment, and have a *positive* self-image based on a healthy balance between self-awareness and self-confidence) before she ever dares to pass judgment on others and on their inability to start the same personal quest. It may be that deep down inside, Susan was not convinced of the advantages to approaching life and work through a deep immersion into her consciousness, and this may have inadvertently transuded to her own team.

We need to make sure that the first person we give any advice to is ourselves and that our standards should be much higher for ourselves than for our teams. As Guanzi wrote, "If a person rises to a level of authority that exceeds his or her virtue, all will suffer."[1] Susan's team will need to see the change in her first, and only after seeing the change will they be willing to accept her advice.

The higher the leader's level of self-awareness, the higher the level of self-awareness his or her team will have. On the other hand, the team as a whole never will be able to exceed the leader's level of awareness. Sometimes there may be exceptional cases of individual employees who possess extremely good insight. Unfortunately, the level of awareness of the whole team is not just the sum of its individual members, and many times these outstanding employees will eventually leave or be expelled from the team. There are many things Susan could do to help her team perform more effectively, and most of them start with focusing on *her* personal development.

Moving from the Self-Awareness Ring into the Team-Awareness Ring

If Susan wants to become a conscious leader, she needs to find a higher purpose in the business, which should align with her own purpose and be something people can relate to while working on theirs. This *team* (or company) purpose is the reason for its existence and the foundation of true organizational engagement, catalyzing the energies of the team members toward the achievement of this final goal. The identification of a common purpose is the first step a leader needs to take to move from the inner self-awareness ring into the team-awareness ring, fueling passion and work ethic among his or her team.

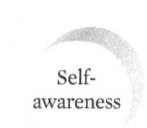

Self-awareness

Team-awareness

Community-awareness

A conscious leader is the one who, after finding a higher purpose in the business by

49

cultivating a *culture* that fosters the increased level of awareness in his or her own team members, instills in them the will to lead themselves by finding their own purposes. The conscious leader promotes a *conscious culture*, which connects him or her with the team, the team members with the company purpose and with each other, and finally the company with its various stakeholders. A conscious culture activates the individual and group reflection, interconnecting and integrating the otherwise dissociated parts that exist within us and with the external world.

The Three Ps of the Team-Awareness Ring

A common vision (*purpose*), shared values (*principles*), and aligned behaviors (*practices*) are the hallmarks of a conscious culture. It is the duty of a conscious leader to bring people together around these three elements. The level of team awareness is affected not only by the common vision but also by the beliefs and behaviors that are expected from and implicitly or explicitly acknowledged by the members. Most companies have beautifully crafted visions and a nice list of values they proclaim they believe in (e.g., honesty, a high level of business ethics, a focus on people, respect for diversity, and so on), but unfortunately, many times there is a discrepancy between the vision and the behaviors. Furthermore, company values sometimes do not transcend the communication statements, and actual behaviors differ significantly from the proclaimed beliefs. Sean's story is a good example of this schizophrenic picture.

This company particularly attracted Sean at his university's job fair. The company's annual report showed its mission and values, which he could fully relate to. This world-renowned consulting firm had the well-being of patients at the heart of its mission, and its core values (honesty and openness, ethics, and comradeship) were pretty much the same as the ones he had been brought up with. Fresh from college, Sean had little experience in the real world, but he was smart enough not to make the mistake of converting his ideals into expectations. Still, his first experiences in the company were much worse than what he would have ever anticipated. Backstabbing was not only a frequent work practice but was even tolerated by senior management. ("It's just business," they would say.) Companionship was frowned upon, and constantly challenging your peers was openly rewarded, while showing a preference for people over business derailed a career. Sean's father had made a huge effort to send him to a good college, and now it was time for Sean to pay it back. He had to make it. He had to have a successful career, even if that meant relinquishing his own internal values. Sean did make it through the middle-management ranks, but it took a toll on his health. He started to get sick often, missing many work days and letting his healthier colleagues take advantage of his absences to steal some of his good ideas and show them to their bosses while they complained to them about Sean's low level of commitment. Eventually Sean was dismissed from his job on the grounds of poor performance and lack of initiative. This company had a huge misalignment between the written values and the actual practices, and this schizophrenic behavior impacted negatively on Sean's satisfaction with his job and, thus, affected his performance negatively.

Unconscious Company Culture

Many companies operate on dog-eat-dog principles, and some famous consulting firms are a good example of this practice. Everyone depends on his or her immediate superior's approval for survival. Failure is punished swiftly and decisively. There is a steady stream of people who enter and exit—fast. Some survive and join the ranks of the others who can tolerate the climate. Most people seem to lead a miserable life in this environment, but still, business supposedly does very well. How is this possible?

The mainstay of this operation is its selection–retention system. People who do not like the environment barely last a few months (Sean), and the ones who stay seem to enjoy the high-energy environment (Wall

Street traders). It may be possible for a company to be highly profitable and keep its employees (the ones who manage to remain) happy without coming even close to the communitarian ideal. But is this type of business healthy and sustainable? What are the hazards it creates for its people and its business prospects? The omen is not good, and its fortune can be bright only in the short term. The talented people it will need to move on to its next stage of development will find the environment to be lacking in congeniality. This type of firm is doubly vulnerable because of the breakdown of its internal culture and the failure of its external adaptivity. It is vulnerable to destructive internal conflicts, and if the market requires a different way of operating, it would find the adjustment difficult to achieve. It might be surviving, but would you invest in a firm with such a long-term horizon? I am deeply convinced that the long-term prospects are best in places that create the values of a true community, in which many kinds of people can be fulfilled by feeling and being personally effective.

The good thing about these dog-eat-dog types of companies is that at least they are true to what they preach—what you see is what you get. You know that if you want to work as a financial trader on Wall Street, you will need to compromise other values in life. The problem is when companies invest a lot of time and money on beautifully crafted visions/missions/values that are the opposite of what they actually do or how they reward their employees. Here are some real-life examples of visions from companies that have recently undergone significant downsizings and in which top managers are still making big bonuses:

- "Our people are our best-valued assets."
- "We put people first."
- "Our mission is to improve the quality of life of our community."
- "We care."

This *schizophrenic* behavior is widespread, and many people seem to say one thing but behave in a completely different way. I have discussed the need to integrate your dissociated self and to integrate your dissociated team members. Many times the *subtle* (and sometimes explicit) messages we receive at work seem to point in a totally opposite direction than the direction included in the company's vision. This is one of the main battles a conscious leader needs to fight: aligning as closely as possible the three Ps: purpose, principles, and practices. It is a journey worth taking, but it presents us with obstacles, many of which are self-imposed, as well as ethical, dilemmas.

Chapter Six

PRINCIPLES IN A CONSCIOUS CULTURE

Oh yes, I'm the great pretender
Adrift in a world of my own
I play the game but to my real shame
You've left me to dream all alone
Too real is this feeling of make believe
Too real when I feel what my heart can't conceal.
—Buck Ram, "The Great Pretender"

Ethical Behavior

We may have the illusion (or the wish) that people rise to places of authority merely on meritorious grounds: competence or technical skills, an ability to make things happen, a sound track record of outstanding results, etc. Unfortunately, particularly in large corporations, many people rise to positions of power on totally different grounds, such as their political ability to play games and their high level of ambition. In the short term, these types of managers may survive, but sooner or later, their lack of integrity comes to light. The problem here is that very little is done in our corporations to develop ethical standards in our leaders. There may be an ethical code and a list of values each person should adhere to, but little attention is paid to how virtue develops in a manager, why some people develop integrity and others do not, or why some people have a deep level of understanding and self-awareness while others have none. Little is done when a person does not command genuine respect or is not credible.

For instance, we demand that our employees respect an ethical code of conduct, but sometimes we do not apply the same principles to our *own* conduct. Or we become blinded to our ethical lapses, a symptom of a poor level of self-awareness. We unconsciously fool ourselves and believe we are more ethical than we actually are. The point here is that we are so busy focusing our attention on making the bottom line, regaining lost market share, etc., that the ethical implications of some decisions we make fade from our minds. Again and again we are not *present* in the moment, and we end up engaging in or condoning behavior that we would condemn if we were consciously aware of it. We assess ourselves in a biased way, and often our confidence in our own integrity is frequently overrated...a good reason why we need an outside, unbiased, and expert observer who can help us identify these blind spots.

Walk the Talk

While teaching at the Lyceum, the famous Aristotle used to stroll about the gardens in the mornings with his regular students discussing philosophy. (The Greek descriptive word for "walking about" came to be applied to the school itself. Thus the school was "peripatetic," and its students and adherents were "peripatetics.") It seems that the modern saying, "If you're going to talk the talk, you've got to walk the walk," stems from this concept. (Other versions that we might have heard in our childhood—including "Actions speak louder than words," "Practice what you preach," and, "Walk it like you talk it"—may make even more sense to us.)

As business leaders, we are always reminded to walk the talk if we want to engage our employees; nobody will follow our directions if we do not practice what we preach, but very few actually manage to do this. It seems that most credible leaders are the ones who are most succinct, because the more you talk, the greater the possibility that you will not practice everything you say. Make sure that the first person you are talking to is not a member of your team but *yourself* when you deliver speeches.

Listen very carefully to your words, and always check for consistency—both in your public and private life. Back to Socrates's philosophy: "The way to gain a good reputation is to endeavor to be what you desire to appear." Unless you are quite certain you are actually practicing some behaviors, avoid dwelling in muddy waters that will otherwise have a counterproductive effect.

Diversity

Companies make a lot of fuss about having the right number of foreigners, women, and minorities on their management teams. They proclaim that they are color-blind and that discrimination on any grounds (nationality, gender, sexual orientation, race, religion, etc.) is not only prohibited but also will be severely punished. Employees attend diversity workshops, minority quotas are established and monitored, and questions about one's personal life are strongly discouraged. The problem here is that diversity is tolerated only on superficial grounds and is not really accepted and celebrated. Thus, people are expected to be different provided that those external differences do not translate into actual different behaviors that can divert from what is established by the unique company culture. Introverts are expected to behave as extroverts, women should have the same leadership style as men, homosexuals should not display affection in public, foreigners should adhere to the same values and life priorities as nationals, single people are expected to stay at work longer that their married colleagues, etc. By just *tolerating* diversity, one misses all of its benefits. As Audre Lorde[1] said, "Difference must be not merely tolerated but seen as a fund of necessary polarities between which our creativity can spark like a dialectic. Only then does the necessity for interdependence become unthreatening." Otherwise, mere toleration implies that minorities enjoy their inherent rights by the indulgence of the majority. Companies will accept those who are different provided that they behave like everyone else.

People First

For most companies, people are the most valued assets, and caring for their well-being and professional development is top priority. Still, rarely is the human-resource director considered to be the most important member of the management committee. The weight that human-resource matters have on the company scorecard is limited; people matters are often placed at the end of the agenda of strategic meetings; and the training budget is the one that gets cut immediately when a company is faced with budget constraints. In reality, we act as if businesses do not depend on the decisions of and interactions between human beings but are only an outcome of economic variables. People are thus considered mere replaceable parts of an abstract entity called "company," as if this was not just the sum of individual human beings. The company unconsciously becomes blind and creates denial. It assumes no value in human connections and actually creates separation by creating more insecurity in employees, resulting in a vicious cycle of increasing insecurity and separateness (and, most likely, performance issues). A conscious leader's job is to view people not as mere assets (who can be used and abused) nor even as resources (who can get depleted), but as *sources* of infinite possibilities that need nurturing and care.

Family and Work Balance

Achieving a healthy balance between personal and professional commitments seems to be placed among the top priorities of human resource departments, and many efforts are carried out to compensate for the time spent at the office (remote work, flexible working schedules, paternity leave, and the like). The funny thing is that the ones who are allowed to enjoy these types of benefits are the rank and file, but very rarely do we see organizations in which leaders (or highfliers) apply real attention to this balance. The subtle schizophrenic message here is that people who want to have a serious career will have to suppress their inner true selves for the sake of professional success. A twenty-four-hour attention to business is required, and investing time in relationships, either outside of work or even at the office, is considered a waste of time. People will see what you do and not hear what you say, so it is the leader's duty to behave according to what he or she preaches and to strike a healthy balance between personal and professional matters.

Authenticity in Business

The divorce between meaning and business fosters pathological behaviors in our employees. People are considered disposable, and relationships suffer. Human interactions are based solely on self-interest and competition. The trip up the corporate ladder becomes lonely, and it feels even lonelier when one reaches the top. A good example of this tragedy can be found in Leo Tolstoy's novella, *Death of Ivan Ilyich*:

> It is as if I had been going downhill while I imagined I was going up. And that is really what it was. I was going up in public opinion, but to the same extent life was ebbing away from me. And now it is all done and there is only one death...The question suddenly occurred to him: "What if my whole life has really been wrong?" It occurred to him that what had appeared perfectly impossible before, namely that he had not spent his life as he should have done, might after all be true. It occurred to him that his scarcely perceptible attempts to struggle against what was considered good by the most highly placed people, those scarcely noticeable impulses which he had immediately suppressed, might have been the real thing, and all the rest false. And his professional duties and the whole arrangement of his life and of his family, and all his social and official interests, might all have been false. He tried to defend all those things to himself and suddenly felt the weaknesses of what he was defending. There was nothing to defend.[2]

Tolstoy masterfully dissects the basic needs, emotions, and motives of people searching for self-knowledge. His character, Ivan Ilyich, exquisitely describes the existential conflicts of a Russian bureaucrat when confronted with his own death and the futility of a life made out of all the proper steps to secure a *successful* career and life. When his death was announced, the thought that it was Ivan who had died and not them consoled his working colleagues, and they could not help but think of the promotions and transfers that Ivan's death would occasion. Ivan Ilyich led what Tolstoy called an "artificial life," which is marked by shallow relationships, self-interest, and materialism. Ivan Ilyich just wanted to take the appropriate steps—both professionally and personally—that would guide him into the right life. But this artificial life composed of carefully planned moves deprived his life of all authentic emotions and deep relationships. It is a deception that hides life's true meaning and leaves one terrified and alone at the moment of death. In an artificial life, one sees others as *a means to an end* instead of seeing them as individual beings with unique thoughts, feelings, and desires. The *authentic* life cultivates mutually affirming human relationships that break down isolation and allow for true interpersonal contact. Whereas the artificial life leaves one alone and empty, the authentic life fosters strength through solidarity and comfort through empathy. It creates true bonds, something that Ivan Ilyich did not manage to do in either his professional or his personal life.

I have listed some of the values (*principles*) we want to instill in and share with our people, which make the foundation for a strong conscious culture in our organizations. But for these values to be ingrained in us first and in our people afterward, we need to translate them into actual behaviors (*practices*) consciously, thus, creating a virtuous circle between both of them. The next chapter presents some concrete examples of putting our values into practice.

Chapter Seven

PRACTICES IN A CONSCIOUS CULTURE

Heal the world
Make it a better place
For you and for me
And the entire human race
There are people dying
If you care enough for the living
Make it a better place
For you and for me.
—Michael Jackson, "Heal the World"

Integrating Performance and Behaviors

Many company leaders state that their most important asset is people and that priority number one is to care for the well-being of the employees and for their personal and professional growth. They care for a healthy and collaborative working environment in which people feel at ease speaking up and are able to develop their potential fully. Still, and returning to the need to walk the talk, in these same companies, very rarely will a high-performing manager be fired because of behavior. A dictatorial style will be tolerated when results are happening; it is only when performance starts to fail that we focus on those signals of poor behavior that were previously dismissed or were covered up by the good results. During the good times, we are blindfolded and unable, as leaders, to spot behavioral flaws that will eventually undermine team cohesiveness and performance. The same happens in politics; it is likely that people will reelect a candidate during the good times, despite signs of ethical issues. Only when the economy starts to get worse do we pay more attention to the *soft* stuff.

When we rate competencies, we put the *learning to do* (getting results) in a different category than the *learning to live together with*. On the measurement tools that we use to rate managers' performance, we rate only outcomes (turnover, operating profit growth, market-share gains, etc.). Sometimes, when we include human-resource targets, their weight (and, thus, their focus) is minimal, and moreover, they rate processes and not behaviors (human-resource turnover rates, number of training courses for employees, number of internal promotions, etc.). Therefore, if we really intend to walk the talk when making performance appraisals, we need to make sure we rate behaviors (emotional intelligence, resilience, quality of interpersonal relationships, ability to manage conflicts, etc.) appropriately and not measure only quantitative (*measurable*) items.

It is, of course, of utmost importance for the survival of any company that financial targets are met, and the trick here is *integrating* performance and behaviors. For instance, the reason we want to track behavior is that we are convinced that, sooner or later, these aspects will eventually impact performance. The longer the time span we use to rate financial performance, the more importance we place on behavior. (It is thus advisable to tie bonuses to consistent performance over several years.) When rating emotional intelligence or resilience, even though some surveys can help, the leader's subjective appraisal will prevail. This is another reason why we should focus first on increasing our level of self-awareness before we attempt to judge others. The better our insight into our own strengths and weaknesses, the better we will become at reading our employees' behaviors.

Promoting Healthy Team Interactions

As previously mentioned many times in this book, any change we attempt to create in our organizations will have to start from us, business leaders, through an increased level of self-awareness. By leading an authentic life and preaching with our personal example, we will be able to spark a similar interest and behavior in the teams we lead. An effective way to promote better and more authentic group relationships is to get to know your team better and let them know you better. A good exercise to get to know your team in a more profound way (and help them increase their level of consciousness) is to start asking them what they really want from their jobs, using Jacques Lacan's theory[1] of needs, wants, and desires:

- **Need** is a biological instinct that is articulated in demand. Needs are related to survival and usually refer to things associated with the physical body. (Money is included in this category.)
- **Demand** has a double function—on the one hand, it articulates need, and on the other, it acts as a demand for love. It is then connected to the realm of affection, affiliation, etc. The demands that employees place on us for recognition, constructive feedback, etc., belong in this category.
- **Desire** is neither the appetite for satisfaction nor the demand for love "but the difference that results from the subtraction of the first from the second." Lacan adds that "desire begins to take shape in the margin in which demand becomes separated from need." It deals with a deeper level of consciousness and involves the profound being of the person.

Building Deep Relationships

Susan's team was wary of any interference in their personal lives, and team members were protective of their private space. Afraid of being judged or discriminated against, nobody wanted to expose to the group any aspect of personality that would make them vulnerable to criticism. Everyone assumed that the only way to increase the effectiveness of the group, and ultimately the long-term sustainability of the company, was to focus on technical—professional—matters. They would welcome any workshop that was intended to develop their skills, provided it did not interfere in any *personal* matters. It was as if nobody had any personal issue—as if each was a sane and fully developed adult, with no childhood issues, personal traumas, or flaws. Because this, of course, is not true for everybody, some psychology had to be introduced into the workplace, but it had to be done under a *professional* disguise, such as the Myers–Briggs assessment.

The Myers–Briggs Type Indicator® (MBTI) assessment, based on Carl Jung's[2] typological theories, is a psychometric questionnaire designed to measure preferences in how people perceive the world and make decisions. Many companies use it as a predictor of job success. Jung proposed the existence of two cognitive functions: rational, or judging (thinking and feeling), and irrational, or perceiving (sensing and intuition). The MBTI sorts some of these differences into four opposite pairs, or dichotomies, with a resulting sixteen possible types, referred to by an abbreviation of the initial letters of each of the four type preferences. For instance, ESTJ stands for extraversion (E), sensing (S), thinking (T), and judgment (J), and INFP stands for introversion (I), intuition (N), feeling (F), and perception (P). Many of us have been labeled according to the way we score on these four aspects. Human-resource experts told us that these different labels would help us work better together, and most us felt pretty safe wearing these labels because they did not actually expose our intimate personalities/wishes/needs but just focused on the way we approach problems and people at work. We would always be dealing with *professional* but not *personal* stuff. No preference or total type is considered better or worse than another, but unfortunately, many companies distorted this tool and used it to screen future employees during job interviews. ("Our executive team is made up of all ESTJs, so we cannot hire an INFP if we want to maintain team cohesiveness.") The assumption behind this was that most of a team's problems would stem from mixing different personality styles. One of the undesired consequences was that many people aspiring to certain jobs started to fake answers to create a sociable accepted personality style. (ESTJs seem to be the prevailing style for leadership positions.)

Honoring Emotion and Motivational Forces

We need to accept the importance and unavoidability of emotion and develop ways of helping people work through rather than against their feelings. We, therefore, need leaders with high levels of emotional intelligence who can spot the wisdom that lies underneath those emotions. We then need to provide these leaders with appropriate tools to identify the drivers behind the manifest behaviors of their employees and, an accurate 360-degree survey that can help understand why leaders and employees do what they do and why they behave in certain ways is a good start.

Manfred Kets De Vries, professor of leadership development at INSEAD, developed an extremely effective assessment tool called Inner Theater Inventory˚. According to him, each person has a *unique theater* that dictates the specific outlook toward the world. I then want to use a play from Spanish writer Pedro Calderón de la Barca (1600–1681), *Life Is a Dream,* to illustrate his point. *Life Is a Dream,* is a philosophical allegory regarding the human situation and the mystery of life; in it, the main character, Segismund, prince of Poland, is imprisoned by his father, the king, because it is prophesied that Segismund would become a tyrant. At the end of the First Act, Segismund, reflecting on his life's condition, says his famous soliloquy on the opposition between destiny and liberty on the topic of life as a dream:

> We live, while we see the sun, where life and dreams are as one. And living has taught me this, man dreams the life that is his, until his living is done. The king dreams he is king, and he lives in the deceit of a king, commanding and governing. And all the praise he receives is written in wind and leaves a little dust on the way, when death ends all with a breath. Where then is the gain of a throne that shall perish and not be known in the other dream that is death? Dreams the rich man of riches and fears, the fears that his riches breed. The poor man dreams of his need, and all his

sorrows and tears. Dreams he that prospers with years, dreams he that feigns and foregoes. Dreams he that rails on his foes. And in all the world, I see, man dreams whatever he be, and his own dream no man knows. And I too dream and behold, I dream I am bound with chains. And I dreamed that these present pains were fortunate ways of old. What is life? A tale that is told. What is life? A frenzy extreme, a shadow of things that seem. And the greatest good is but small. That all life is a dream to all, and that dreams themselves are a dream.

When commenting on his own play, Pedro Calderón de la Barca expressed that people behaved like actors of a theater play called *Life*. Proffesor De Vries talks about a somewhat similar theory of a thematic imagery in people's own inner theatre—the scripts—which determines their way of interpreting the world and influences their behaviors and actions. His Inner Theater Inventory* (ITI) is a 360-degree survey instrument that helps understand why people do what they do and why they behave in certain ways: the *inner scripts* help people make meaning out of their experiences and influence what they value. Professor De Vries believes that, in order to identify the drivers of people's inner theatre, it is not sufficient to look at just manifest behavior; the observations should take into account underlying *motivational forces*. These forces affect not only the relationship with peers, subordinates, and bosses but also the overall management style and decision-making processes. Henceforth, it is imperative to cultivate self-awareness to better understand why people do what they do and what it is that makes them tick, getting in touch with their inner set of values, beliefs, and behavior that ultimately guide their actions. The Inner Theater Inventory questionnaire is designed to help executives understand and use the feedback they receive to develop a greater sense of self-awareness and, thus, a lifestyle more congruent with their values and belief systems.

Some other companies (even though this is much more common in academia), recognizing human complexity have gone a step further, adopting a *transdisciplinary approach*[3] that proposes four characteristics for each individual that will determine personal success:

1. **Learning to know**—this is the ability to have access to the knowledge the world has to offer and the ability to incorporate it. It is directly correlated to a person's IQ.
2. **Learning to do**—this means acquiring a profession and implementing the knowledge incorporated into our lives. It deals with experience, and it can sometimes be spotted just from looking at a person's résumé. Because both of these pillars deal with *professional* characteristics, they are broadly accepted in our corporate world as measures of success.
3. **Learning to be**—this deals with our level of self-awareness and with the harmony or disharmony between our individual life and social life.
4. **Learning to live together**—this is the ability to accept another person's opinions, to negotiate between the ins and outs of conflicts, and to respect and embrace people's differences.

These last two aspects are less popular in our corporations because they deal with softer, more *personal* stuff, and managers are less prone to accept them and incorporate them into their developmental efforts with their teams. The above-mentioned transdisciplinary approach is, thus, based on an *equilibrium* between the exterior person and the interior person. In this context, it integrates the professional aspects (to know and to do) with the personal ones (to be and to live together). We need to place at least as much emphasis on developing the necessary skills to help our employees increase their level of self-awareness and emotional maturity as we do on developing the *hard* qualities.

I must confess that I am not a big fan of the old saying, "Angel of the pavement, devil at home." It is my experience that employees can rarely dissociate their work life from their personal life. A person brings his or her whole self to work, and the way he or she interacts with family and friends will mimic work relationships and his or her relationship with authority. It is not a question of getting into the private life of the individual employee but of acknowledging the role the *personal* part plays on an individual who is part of a team. Unless we thoroughly invest in these aspects and go beyond the dichotomy between the hard and soft stuff, we will not be able to make a quantum leap in the effectiveness of our groups. Unfortunately, because the fallacy of not accepting as real what cannot be measured is pretty common, it is easy to relegate the soft stuff, such as people's sense of purpose in their work (related to the ability to be) and the quality of interpersonal relationships (related to the ability to live together with), to a secondary status.

It is our task as leaders to dive into the *personal* sphere and instill in our employees the wish to delve into their own self-awareness. The best way to accomplish this is to walk the talk. By showing our interest in increasing our own level of self-awareness—exposing our weaknesses as well as our strengths, explicitly communicating our purpose in life, working with professionally trained psychologists (instead of coaches, who often deal only with external behavioral changes that are not sustainable in the long term)—we will awaken in our teams the desire to embark on this personal quest.

Complex as it may seem, there are some easy initial steps you can take to be personal without exposing yourself to potential trouble:

- **Get personal when interviewing candidates**—you can very well avoid questions about race, religion, marital status, or politics and avoid infringing any code of conduct and still get personal. You can get to know candidates from a personal point of view by asking questions that have to do more with values: what drives them, what they consider important in their lives, what their ultimate goal is, which of the values they most respect in the people who surround them, etc.

- **Promote face-to-face interactions**—in the world of social media, it is easy to stay connected to your friends or working colleagues. Out of fear of exposing ourselves too much, we use e-mail as a shield. We are safe in delivering objective messages to our teams without the risk of exposing any sentimental components. Technology allows us to avoid tone, shades, nonverbal language, or anything that can reveal what we actually think and *feel*. But in spite of our efforts, people will always interpret our written messages—many times in the wrong way. It is, therefore, advisable to encourage face-to-face meetings and even video and phone calls over e-mail. Here are some concrete tips: Reduce the size of team members' in-boxes to discourage e-mail; create internal e-mail-free Fridays; and adapt your office layout by rotating work spaces, eliminating closed offices, and turning the best spaces into meeting rooms.
- **Bring in social leaders as external speakers**—they can help get people out of their comfort zone by discussing matters that are (supposedly) not related to business. In that setting, people may feel more comfortable about speaking up and expressing their views on matters that affect society as a whole. (Of course, try to avoid bringing in politicians and religious leaders.)
- **When benchmarking successful companies, discuss the psychological aspects of industry leaders, showing what their values are and what makes them tick.**

Spotting and Uprooting Negative Behaviors

Many times, organizations make us do the things that come naturally to us in an unnatural way. This creates a tension. We make a mess of managing people because we try to do things according to the rule book—following the constraints of our business world—and suppress any type of emotions. We dismiss our feelings and try to act only on external behaviors, with the false illusion that people will not notice our real intentions. And it is in this type of environment that certain personality disorders may thrive, like *the company sociopath*.

A sociopath is someone *without* a conscience. It is someone who does not feel or need affection, who does not care about others, and who deceives and hurts people without any trace of remorse. Sociopaths don't feel guilty or sorry for any pain they may inflict on others. They climb the corporate ladder, taking what they want on their way up. Unfortunately, many of them are pretty intelligent and astute observers, and they have learned how to mimic feelings of affection and empathy remarkably well. For that reason, sociopaths can go undetected as they wreak havoc on people they work with. It is estimated that about 1 percent of the general population are sociopaths. (Some researchers put the figure at 3 or 4 percent.) The percentage goes much higher in certain types of environments in which power over people is exerted, like big corporations or politics.

In his book *Without Conscience: The Disturbing World of the Psychopaths Among Us*[4], Robert Hare depicts the character traits of these people with clear examples. Even though most of his work has been done in prisons, it is frightening how much these people have in common with the types of ugly bosses or peers many of us have unfortunately met or worked with. His definition of psychopathology includes these criteria:

- Comes across as smooth, polished, and charming
- Turns most conversations around to a discussion of himself or herself
- Discredits and puts down others in order to build up his or her own image and reputation
- Lies to coworkers, customers, or business associates with a straight face
- Considers people he or she has outsmarted or manipulated as dumb or stupid
- Opportunistic—hates to lose, plays ruthlessly to win
- Comes across as cold and calculating
- Acts in an unethical or dishonest manner

- Has created a power network in the organization and uses it for personal gain
- Shows no regret for making decisions that negatively affect the company, shareholders, or employees

It may be that when managers send employees to seminars on *managing* people that teach forced external behaviors without paying due attention to actual intentions, they are unwittingly nurturing sociopaths in their organizations. Let's take some of the characteristics sociopaths have and look at how they could be considered leadership qualities: polished and cool decisiveness (decision-making skills?); fondness for the fast lane (promotion potential?); cunning manipulation of people (people-management skills?); and lack of remorse (rebound-from-failure skills?). It is not that rare for companies to mistake these character traits as *leadership* qualities and, thus, single out these special people for promotion. That is why Robert Hare believes sociopaths are increasingly common in business. Like bees to honey, these people are particularly attracted to the pace and volatility of today's hypercompetitive workplaces.

There are ways to spot a sociopath within your organization. Hare mentions some of the things companies can do to contain sociopaths or expel them from work:

- Make it easy for rank-and-file workers to express concerns about colleagues. Have an ombudsman or an anonymous tip line. Because regular employees are less useful to a sociopath than leaders are, the sociopath's mask will often come off in front of staff, and employees will pick up on a psychopath's game before management does.
- Thoroughly cross-check your impressions of your high-potential employees with colleagues who know them well. A sociopath will tell you exactly what you want to hear, and it may be quite different from what he or she tells others. When the stories don't align, take a closer look.

- Finally, and most importantly, work on your level of consciousness—on your self-awareness. As mentioned previously, leaders are famously conscious of their strengths (self-confidence) but often clueless about their vulnerabilities (self-awareness). A sociopath will manipulate you by exploiting your personal weaknesses. Learn about your weaknesses (remember also the SWOT analysis for your team), and beware when someone seeks advantage by playing to them.

Apart from Hare's suggestion on how to spot—and contain—a sociopath, there is a key element that you personally need to tackle first: When interacting with your colleagues, start *from the inside out* (internal feelings first, external behavior afterward). Work first on your deep intentions, on your convictions, and on your purpose, and deal with them. Work on your behaviors *only* afterward. Once you are deeply convinced of your purpose at work, of the importance that your colleagues have in this quest, and in their own need for self-realization in what they do, then and only then will the proper verbal and nonverbal language follow through naturally and spontaneously. It is from that moment on that you will be treating your employees like real human beings and not as stepping stones on your way up (or down). Do your best to make your behavior resemble more of the traits of Pickering's than the one from phonetics professor Henry Higgins in George Bernard Shaw's play *Pygmalion*.[5]

The Pygmalion Effect

The Pygmalion, or Rosenthal, effect refers to the phenomenon in which the greater the expectation placed on people, often children or students (employees in our case), the better they perform. The effect is named after Pygmalion, a Cypriot sculptor in a narrative by Ovid in Greek mythology who fell in love with a female statue he had carved out of ivory. The Pygmalion effect is a form of self-fulfilling prophecy, and, in this respect, people with poor expectations internalize their negative label, and those with positive labels succeed accordingly.

Within sociology, the effect is often cited with regard to education and social class. More recently, in George Bernard Shaw's *Pygmalion*, Professor Henry Higgins insists he can take a cockney flower girl and, with some rigorous training, pass her off as a duchess. He succeeds, but a key point lies in a comment made by her trainee, Eliza Doolittle, to Higgins's friend, Pickering: "You see, really and truly, apart from the things anyone can pick up (the dressing and the proper way of speaking and so on), the difference between a lady and a flower girl is not how she behaves but how she's treated. I shall always be a flower girl to Professor Higgins, because he always treats me as a flower girl, but I know I can be a lady to you because you always treat me as a lady, and you always will." Pickering surely did not go through any course on mastering verbal and nonverbal language, but he honestly believed in treating this girl as a lady, and his verbal and nonverbal language was naturally consistent with his inner thoughts.

The higher your level of consciousness, the higher the level of the team's and the better you will become at managing people in a truthful manner—understanding what really motivates people and the limits to change. We want to avoid the quick solutions that some behavioral programs present (one-size-fits-all type of recommendations), which do not consider that individuals react differently according to their unique character biases. The path is longer but much more sustainable in the long term. We need to be true to how we actually feel about our employees and act accordingly, without manipulating people into fulfilling our own wishes. For instance, we cannot change a person, but we can change the image that he or she has of us. By internally changing what we think and feel about a person, this person will notice that some of our behaviors have changed, and he or she *may* change as a result. I am not saying that this is going to happen all of the time, but I personally believe it is more likely that you will be able to sustain an honest working relationship when you start with your internal feelings and act as a consequence of this change instead of artificially trying to behave in a certain way and portraying a fake image to win people's confidence.

I have discussed some examples of how we can build a strong conscious culture by putting shared desired behaviors in practice. We can promote more honest working relationships by being true to ourselves and to our purpose first, before attempting to ask for the same in our employees. Even if we follow the right sequence, some people will be willing to find their purpose in life, and some will not. Even if we do our utmost, some people will not want to deal with their self-awareness. Our job consists of instilling in our people the need to be their own leaders, but it should stop there. Our mission as leaders is to hand over to our teams the necessary tools, but it will be completely up to our employees to accept and use them. We are leaders in the business of managing people, but there is a fine line between honestly trying to develop the best in our people so that they become better leaders and coercing people into doing what we want. Furthermore, the intent is not to invade your employees' intimate personal lives but to understand what drives each one of them. You can always stay within the work environment and still construct more honest and profound relationships among your team members, integrating them at a more spiritual level (in terms of *meaning*, not religion). This close connection will facilitate the move toward the third ring of conscious leadership, which is connecting you and your group with the community you operate in to achieve a deeper level of *community awareness*.

PART FOUR

THE COMMUNITY-
AWARENESS RING

Chapter Eight

COMPANY CONSCIOUSNESS

You think you own whatever land you land on
The earth is just a dead thing you can claim
But I know every rock and tree and creature
Has a life, has a spirit, has a name.
You think the only people who are people
Are the people who look and think like you
But if you walk the footsteps of a stranger
You'll learn things you never knew you never knew.
—Stephen Schwartz, "Colors of the Wind"

According to UNICEF, 22,000 children die each day due to poverty. Around 27 to 28 percent of all children in developing countries are estimated to be underweight or experience stunted growth. The two regions that account for the bulk of the deficit are South Asia and sub-Saharan Africa. If current trends continue, the Millennium Development Goals' target of halving the proportion of underweight children will be missed by 30 million children, largely because of slow progress in South Asia and sub-Saharan Africa. One of every two children in the world (one billion) lives in poverty.

The poorest 40 percent of the world's population accounts for 5 percent of global income. The richest 20 percent accounts for three-quarters of the world's income. More than 80 percent of the world's population lives in countries where income differentials are widening.

Water problems affect half of humanity. Some 1.1 billion people in developing countries have inadequate access to water, and 2.6 billion lack basic sanitation. Also, 1.8 billion people who have access to a water source within one kilometer, but not in their house or yard, consume around twenty liters per day. In the United Kingdom, the average person uses more than fifty liters of water a day flushing toilets (where average daily water usage is about 150 liters a day). The highest average water use in the world is in the United States, at 600 liters a day. Close to half of all the people in developing countries are suffering at any given time from a health problem caused by water and sanitation deficits.

Indoor air pollution resulting from the use of solid fuels (by poorer segments of society) is a major killer. It claims the lives of 1.5 million people each year, more than half of them below the age of five—that is 4,000 deaths a day. To put this number in context, it exceeds total deaths from malaria and rivals the number of deaths from tuberculosis.

And yet, many of us are doing well.

The Illusion of Fragmentation

Fragmentation is a way of thinking. As David Joseph Bohm[1] explains, it consists of a false division, making a division where there is a tight connection, and seeing separateness where there is wholeness. Bohn called fragmentation—in our view of the universe and of ourselves as separate from one another and nature—"the hidden source of social, political, and environmental crises facing the world." Nature that surrounds us transmits a permanent and eloquent message of interdependence among everything and everyone; still, we behave as if we will be immune to the effects of our actions. We have the illusion of unlimited resources, as if the earth were an unlimited source of commodities that can feed our productive frenzy and consumerism— which, by the way, have contributed to the present economic, social, and environmental crisis we are facing.

We are experiencing a lost battle between two conflicting forces: the clash between our greed and our addiction to endless exponential economic expansion and an unsustainable extraction of resources from the environment. Some people may argue that with technology it is possible to increment productivity and, thus, get more with less—for instance, by producing goods that can eventually be recycled, mankind will be able to continue an exponential consumption of products, regardless of the fixed boundaries the environment presents. But most of us are quite familiar with the law of diminishing returns and know that, despite all of our efforts to become more efficient, we are rapidly reaching a limit to ever-increasing gross domestic product (GDP—by the way, isn't economics the social science of choice under scarcity?), and unless we drastically change the way we interact with nature, we will condemn ourselves to self-destruction.

A good example of the efforts to repair what we human beings have disorganized or destroyed lies in the works of Pierre Weil.[2] He proposes a new method of education that can help integrate ourselves with our environment. He then presents three different concepts of ecology:

- **Individual ecology**—this refers to the relationship between ecology and consciousness, and it concerns the fields of the body, emotions, and spirit, with the final objective of achieving internal peace—peace with oneself.
- **Social ecology**—this refers to the relationship with other human beings, and it concerns the fields of economy, society, politics, and culture, with the objective of achieving peace with other human beings.
- **Global ecology**—this more generally refers to the relationship with the universe in general (consciousness of the universe), and it concerns the fields of matter, life, and information, with the final objective of being in harmony with nature.

Once again, the higher our level of consciousness, the higher the likelihood we will be able to integrate the often dissociated peace within ourselves, the dissociation and fragmentation between us and the people who surround us, and ultimately between all of us and the environment that surrounds us.

Social Responsibility

We have come a long way since that famous article Milton Friedman wrote and published in a 1970 issue of *The New York Times* magazine about social responsibility ("the social responsibility of business is to increase its profits"). The financial community of that time received the article warmly:

> When I hear businessmen speak eloquently about the "social responsibilities of business in a free-enterprise system," I am reminded of the wonderful line about the Frenchman who discovered at the age of seventy that he had been speaking prose all his life. The businessmen believe that they are defending free enterprise when they declaim that business is not concerned "merely" with profit but also with promoting desirable "social" ends; that business has a "social conscience" and takes seriously its responsibilities for providing employment, eliminating discrimination, avoiding pollution, and whatever else may be the catchwords of the contemporary crop of reformers. In fact they are—or would be if they or anyone else took them seriously—preaching pure and unadulterated socialism. Businessmen who talk this way are unwitting puppets of the intellectual forces that have been undermining the basis of a free society these past decades.... In a free-enterprise, private-property system, a corporate executive is an employee of the owners of the business. He has direct responsibility to his employers. That responsibility is to conduct the business in accordance with their desires, which generally will be to make as much money as possible while conforming to the basic rules of the society, both those embodied in law and those embodied in ethical custom.... There is one and only one social responsibility of business—to use its resources and engage in activities designed to increase its profits so long as it stays within the rules of the

game, which is to say, engages in open and free competition without deception or fraud.[3]

Friedman fully described the consequences of *unconscious* business. The lesser the personal insight, the stronger the need to separate mankind into selfish and selfless people. For him, there is an internal fragmentation in each person between the give and take aspects. He sees corporations as sterile Darwinian shark tanks in which the only thing that matters is the bottom line. It is as if adults behave as unconscious children, where sharing always implies a loss, a sacrifice.

Even children are taught better, and organizations like Spirituality For Kids (SFK)[4] are a catalyst for change in our communities. They increase the level of self-awareness of children, integrate their selfish and selfless internal aspects, help them understand the joy of sharing, and help them recognize that the one who gives is actually the one who receives the most. The more conscious we become, the more we move from win–lose transactions to win–win. SFK's approach is based on the development of the concept of Social Emotional Learning (SEL), which provides several benefits to students, including the following:

- **Self-awareness**—recognizing one's emotions; identifying and cultivating one's strengths and positive qualities
- **Self-management**—monitoring and regulating one's emotions; establishing and working toward achieving positive goals
- **Relationship skills**—establishing and maintaining healthy, rewarding relationships based on cooperation, effective communication, conflict resolution, and an ability to resist inappropriate social pressure
- **Responsible decision making**—assessing situational influences and generating, implementing, and evaluating ethical solutions to problems that promote one's own and others' well-being
- **Social awareness**—understanding others' thoughts and feelings and appreciating the value of human differences

The learning approach that SFK uses on children can very well be replicated with adults. (I personally have SFK teachers conduct a workshop with my executive team, and I strongly encourage you to try it.)

Unfortunately, many times the level of consciousness that top managers have does not differ much from the level that children have. It is like, when working your way up the corporate ladder, some unconscious business decisions increase your level of denial and self-deception, making you become less mature and causing you to see the external world as a separate entity with no interconnections.

Conscious Social Responsibility

We are all interconnected and interdependent. If there is social injustice, unfair income distribution, animosity and aggressiveness toward foreigners, etc., it is because we have forgotten that we *belong to each other*. Social responsibility started as a way companies had to give back to the communities they operated in. They tried to behave as good neighbors, which meant first avoiding things that spoil the place they lived in and then moved into a more active role of voluntarily assuming the obligation to help solve neighborhood problems. Unfortunately, this original concept has become distorted, and social responsibility moved toward being just a company-branding concept. Its focus was more on appearing to do something good to improve the company reputation than on the actual desire to make a difference. *Conscious social responsibility*, on the other hand, strives to create value in all of the interdependent entities the company works with. Its actions are characterized by the following:

- The one who benefits from the action is not perceived as inferior, not as a person in need, but as an *interconnected equal partner*. It is critical for both parties to understand one another's thoughts and feelings and to appreciate the value of human differences.

- The actual transaction between the two parties (company and community members) is not a win–lose but a win–win; the relationship creates value for ourselves and for others. It is through the giving and sharing that I can reach my ultimate goal of being "my best me."
- The main effect of interacting with our communities is not necessarily a better company reputation but a more conscious working team with increased empathy and tolerance and increased interpersonal skills, such as active listening, teamwork, and overall leadership skills. Employees are exposed to diverse people and challenging situations, and the sharing that takes place during social-responsibility actions bonds people together at a deeper level of consciousness.

Conscious corporate social responsibility (CCSR) then represents a broad concern with business' role that goes beyond the mere economic targets and much more into the overall improvement of the social order by having a deep concern to solve society's needs and goals. CCSR transcends the well-intentioned activities and sporadic charitable contributions—to be a good neighbor—and implies that the behavior of the corporations should be ethical and congruent with the expectations that society demands. In fact, due to the high exposure and, thus, impact potential businessmen have, they should also possess higher standards of ethical behaviors than citizens at large. CCSR is then a driving force within corporations for a higher level of awareness of the social and environmental effects businesses have and of the potential conflict of interest between the profit motive and the potential benefit/damage on the lives of stakeholders and the external community. In essence, CCSR seeks that businesses should do, as a whole, more good than harm by being conscious of their impact on a human's inner and outer world. Some companies have adopted a triple bottom-line approach, which seeks to look at businesses from a holistic perspective, aiming to achieve financial, environmental, and social goals at the same time.

Community Awareness and Purpose

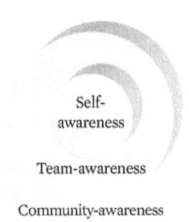

Self-awareness

Team-awareness

Community-awareness

As in the previous two rings, a clearly defined purpose will elevate the level of awareness—this time of the community and the environment we interact with. The inner purpose of the leader, which is shared with and enriched by his or her team, needs to create value for each of those external entities that are influenced by the business. Even competitors are part of the company's stakeholders, and a conscious leader views them not as adversaries to defeat but as interconnected entities that can help the company achieve its purpose by learning from their actions and seeking ways to cooperate together on win–win relationships.

Like with individuals, companies are also striving to make a difference in this world. This effort is defined by a company's purpose, which will help the company attract, retain, and align the right people. There are numerous examples of *purpose* in all kinds of businesses that transcends the mere search for profit and appeals to higher moral qualities. Here are a few:

- To contribute to concrete and relevant changes that lead to more sustainable development in Latin America—Avina Foundation
- To build the best product, cause no unnecessary harm, use business to inspire, and implement solutions to the environmental crisis—Patagonia
- To use our imagination to bring happiness to people—Disney
- To change the lives of people living with diabetes—Novo Nordisk
- To honor the body with conscious choices—Avalon Organics
- To bring color to the lives of people—Coral
- To create sustainable solutions essential to a better, safer, healthier life for people everywhere—DuPont

- To create products and services which promote the well-being of people—Natura
- To cocreate strategies that help businesses grow while generating social value, bridging purpose with profit—Mandalah

Thus, the actual purpose of a company is not that different from the one a single individual can have in his or her own life. We are all trying to make a difference in this world, and companies are not abstract entities but just groups of people united around a common purpose. The level of awareness a company has of its interdependence with the environment and community and of the need to create value to all of them will be dictated by the clarity of its purpose, values, and the level of awareness of its employees. As mentioned previously, the higher the level of awareness the leader has, the higher the level of awareness his or her team members and the company overall will have.

A conscious business is then made of people who are fully aware of the impact their actions have; it is about people who live and work knowing that everything is interconnected, who manage to consciously balance business with social impact. John Mackey—cofounder and CEO of WholeFoods®—started a movement called *Conscious Capitalism*®, which refers to businesses that serve the interest of all constituents who are interdependently linked: customers, employees, investors, communities, suppliers, and the environment. These businesses should have four pillars:

1. **Higher Purpose**—recognizing that every business has a purpose that includes, but is more than, making money. By focusing on its higher purpose, a business inspires, engages, and energizes its stakeholders.
2. **Stakeholder Orientation**—recognizing that the interdependent nature of life and the human foundations of business and that a business needs to create value with and for its various stakeholders (customers, employees, vendors, investors, communities, etc.)

Like the life-forms in an ecosystem, healthy stakeholders lead to a healthy business system.

3. **Conscious Leadership**—human social organizations are created and guided by leaders, or people who see a path and inspire others to travel along the path. Conscious leaders understand and embrace the higher purpose of business and focus on creating value for and harmonizing the interests of the business stakeholders. They recognize the integral role of culture and purposefully cultivate conscious culture.

4. **Conscious Culture**—this is the ethos (the values, principles, and practices) underlying the social fabric of a business, which permeates the atmosphere of a business and connects the stakeholders to each other and to the purpose, people, and processes that comprise the company.

John Mackey was once asked his opinion on Adam Smith's famous quote from his work *An Inquiry into the Nature and Causes of the Wealth of Nations*:

> By pursuing his own interest, man frequently promotes that of the society more effectually than when he really intends to promote it. I have never known much good done by those who affected to trade for the public good.

His answer was that this *invisible hand* of Adam Smith should be supplemented by the *visible hand* of intentional do-goodism and that *conscious* individuals, government, and businesses have endless opportunities to attempt to do good in the world. Henceforth, we are back again to the initial driving force of the change we want to see in society, which starts with you, as an individual conscious leader *taking action*.

PART FIVE

FINAL WORDS

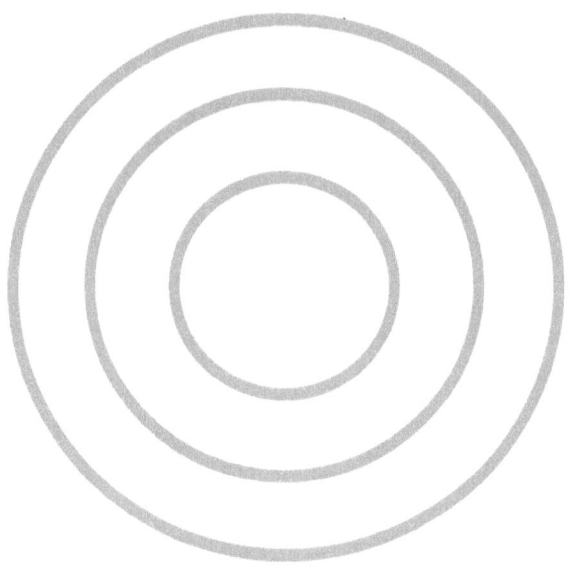

Chapter Nine

TAKE ACTION

I'm starting with the man in the mirror,
I'm asking him to change his ways,
And no message could have been any clearer,
If you wanna make the world a better place,
Take a look at yourself and then make a change.
—Siedah Garrett and Glen Ballard, "Man in the Mirror"

So, what's next? We all share the diagnostic that the world is not moving along the right track, that corruption is pervading all levels of our populations, that environmental crises are getting more frequent and serious, that income disparity is widening, that violence is widespread, that institutions are crumbling, that values are disappearing, that money prevails over people, and that capitalism is not working. But sharing the same diagnostic is not enough. It is easy to be an armchair critic from the comfort of our offices, but it is also very frustrating.

We can change the world. And the only way to do this is to *change ourselves*: to increase our level of self-awareness; to become more aware; to fully understand the impact of our behaviors and actions on others; to accept that we all are interconnected; and to understand the power we have as leaders to instill in others the desire to become conscious leaders themselves. We need to break some habits and recognize and face our fears. We need to become, as Pierre Weill said, the mutants in this world, a new human species created by a higher level of consciousness. We will become the true agents of change:

- **Find your own purpose in life.** As Rabbi Nilton Bonder says, you can spend your whole life looking for a meaning, or you can create a meaning to your life while you live.
- **Help others find their own purpose.** Sometimes this task will already be your own purpose.
- **Be present.** Live intensively in the only thing you have, the present moment, and your enjoyment will encourage the people you lead to do the same.
- **Be assertively humble.** Expose and embrace your weaknesses, which will encourage people to get closer and build intimacy at work; use your strengths to help them deal with their weaknesses.
- **Be ethical.** Promote a conscious culture at work based on strong values and consistent practices. Allow your moral intelligence to prevail.
- **Be socially conscious.** Accept others and the environment as integrated parts of a world conscience to which you belong, and treat them as well as you treat yourself.

We can make a difference, and this difference depends on *you* (not on others) and on your willingness to take ownership and responsibility and to stop victimizing and blaming somebody outside ourselves. Let's accept the fact that the outside world is just a reflection of our own internal conflicts. Each one of us can become more aware. Our own internal change will make the difference. Let's stop blaming others for injustices and take responsibility. Let's confront (but not repress) our fears and take action. Let's embrace our flaws and our inner conflicts. Let's integrate our dissociated selves. Let's make our mark, starting with ourselves, then with our work colleagues, then with the companies we work in, and then with the communities we interact with. Let's change so we can *change the world.*

NOTES

Chapter One. Integrated Leadership Today

1. Michel de Montaigne (1533–1592)—French Renaissance thinker considered to be the inventor of the personal essay. He attempted to weigh or assay his nature, his habits, his own opinions, and those of others. He was a representative of Renaissance skepticism and fideism.
2. Albert Einstein (1879–1955)—German theoretical physicist and developer of the theory of relativity. Won the Nobel Prize for physics in 1921. The quote refers to the fact that we cannot solve our problems with the same thinking we used when we created them.
3. Thomas Hobbes (1588–1679)—English philosopher known for his work on political philosophy. In his book *Leviathan,* he asserts than one learns more by studying oneself, particularly the feelings that influence our thoughts and motivate our actions.

Chapter Two. Goals and Purposes

1. Dorothy Sayers (1893–1957)—English playwright, scholar, and author of mysteries. She also wrote theological essays and published a translation of Dante's epic poem, *The Divine Comedy*.
2. Viktor Frankl (1905–1997)—Austrian neurologist, psychiatrist, and Holocaust survivor. Founder of Logotherapy, which is based on an existential analysis focusing on Kierkegaard's *will to meaning*.
3. Abraham Twerski (1930–)—American psychiatrist, ordained rabbi, and founder and medical director of the Gateway Rehabilitation Center of Aliquippa, Pennsylvania. He is the author of more than

sixty books on Judaism and self-help topics, including several books with Charles M. Schultz's *Peanuts* comic strips used to illustrate human interaction and behavior.

Chapter Three. Job or Career?

1. Siddartha Gautama (birth and death dates uncertain—around 400 BCE)—Indian mystic and founder of Buddhism.
2. Eckhart Tolle (1948–)—German-born spiritual leader and author of *The Power of Now* and *A New Earth*.
3. Allen Saunders (1899–1986)—American writer, journalist, and cartoonist.
4. Socrates (469 BCE–399 BCE)—Greek Athenian philosopher, credited as one of the founders of Western philosophy, known through the accounts of his students Plato and Xenophon and the plays of his contemporary, Aristophanes. He said, "It is not living that matters, but living rightly." Here are some examples of Socrates's life lessons...
   - Be content: "He who is not contented with what he has would not be contented with what he would like to have."
   - Beware of friends who say only kind words: "Think not those faithful who praise all thy words and actions, but those who kindly reprove thy faults."
   - Cultivate the joy of reading: "Employ your time in improving yourself by other men's writings so that you shall gain easily what others have labored hard for."
   - Be the change you want to see: "To do is to be."
   - Gain a good reputation: "The way to gain a good reputation is to endeavor to be what you desire to appear."
   - Speak the truth: "False words are not only evil in themselves, but they infect the soul with evil."

Chapter Four. Self-Awareness and Self-Confidence

1. Daniel Goleman (1946–)—American author, psychologist, and journalist. Author of more than ten books on psychology, education, science, ecological crisis, and leadership.
2. Reinhold Niebuhr (1892–1971)—American Protestant theologian whose social doctrines profoundly influenced American theological and political thought. He was notable primarily for his examination of the interrelationships among religion, individuals, and modern society. He is also the author of "The Serenity Prayer": "God, grant me the serenity to accept the things I cannot change, courage to change the things I can, and wisdom to know the difference. Living one day at a time; enjoying one moment at a time; accepting hardship as a pathway to peace; taking, as Jesus did, this sinful world as it is, not as I would have it; trusting that you will make all things right if I surrender to your will; so that I may be reasonably happy in this life and supremely happy with you forever in the next. Amen."

Chapter Five. Team Awareness

1. *The Guanzi* is an encyclopedic compilation of Chinese philosophical materials named after the seventh-century BCE philosopher Guan Zhong.

Chapter Six. Principles in a Conscious Culture

1. Audre Lorde (1934–1992)—American writer and civil-rights activist who dedicated her life to confronting and addressing the injustices of racism, sexism, and homophobia.
2. Leo Tolstoy (1828–1910)—Russian writer and master of realistic fiction best known for two long novels: *War and Peace* and *Anna Karenina*. *The Death of Ivan Ilyich* is a novella he wrote shortly after his religious conversion in the late 1870s.

Chapter Seven. Practices in a Conscious Culture

1. Jacques Lacan (1901–1981)—French psychoanalyst and psychiatrist.
2. Carl Jung (1875–1961)—Swiss psychiatrist and psychotherapist and founder of analytical psychology.
3. The *transdisciplinary approach* is a framework for allowing members of an educational team to contribute knowledge and skills, collaborate with other members, and collectively determine the services that would benefit a child the most.
4. Robert Hare (1934–)—Canadian researcher in the field of criminal psychology.
5. George Bernard Shaw (1856–1950)—Irish playwright and cofounder of the London School of Economics.

Chapter Eight. Company Consciousness

1. David Joseph Bohm (1917–1992)—American theoretical physicist who contributed innovative and unorthodox ideas to quantum theory, philosophy of mind, and neuropsychology.
2. Pierre Weil (1924–2008)—French psychologist, author, and educator who stated that the goal of holistic education was to repair our self-inflicted ecological disasters and bring back a balance between humankind and our environment.
3. Milton Friedman (1912–2006)—American economist, statistician, and writer who received the 1976 Nobel Memorial Prize in Economic Sciences.
4. Spirituality For Kids, a free online program, helps children tap into their inner strengths and see that the power to overcome any challenge lies within them. By helping kids understand the benefits of human dignity, tolerance, and connecting to self, community, and the world, they are better equipped to become conscious leaders in their homes, schools, and communities. For further information, consult www.spiritualityforkids.com.

BIBLIOGRAPHY

Bergman, Sergio. *Celebrar la Diferencia: Unidad en la Diversidad.* http://www.sergiobergman.com/Libros/celebrar-la-diferencia/.

Bonder, Nilton. *Our Immoral Soul: A Manifesto of Spiritual Disobedience.* Boston: Shambhala Publications, 2001.

Desikachar, T.K.V. *What Are We Seeking?* Chennai, India: Krishnamacharya Yoga Mandiram, 2005.

Frankl, Viktor. *Man's Search for Meaning.* New York: Pocket Books, 1959.

Greenberger, Dennis, and Christine Padesky. *Mind Over Mood: Change How You Feel by Changing the Way You Think.* New York: The Guilford Press, 1995.

Greenleaf, Robert K. *Servant Leadership: A Journey into the Nature of Legitimate Power and Greatness.* Mahwah, NJ: Paulist Press, 1977.

Happé, Robert. *Consciência ê a Resposta* (*Consciousness Is the Answer*). Sao Paulo: Editora Talento, 1997. http://www.roberthappe.net/pages/ingles_book.asp.

Hare, Robert D. *Without Conscience: The Disturbing World of the Psychopaths among Us.* New York: The Guilford Press, 1993.

Jaworski, Joseph. *Synchronicity: The Inner Path of Leadership.* San Francisco: Barrett–Koehler Publishers, Inc., 2011.

Mackey, John, Rajendra Sisoida, and Bill George. *Conscious Capitalism: Liberating the Heroic Spirit of Business*. Boston: Harvard Business School Publishing Corporation, 2013.

Nicolescu, Basarab. *La Transdisciplinarité*. http://www.basarab-nicolescu. fr/BOOKS/TDRocher.pdf.

O'Donnell, Ken. *Pathways to Higher Consciousness: Finding Your True Inner Self*. New York: Sterling Ethos, 2009.

Scharmer, C. Otto. *Theory U: Leading from the Future as It Emerges*. San Francisco: Barrett–Koehler Publishers, Inc., 2009.

Senge, Peter M., C. Otto Scharmer, Joseph Jaworski, and Betty Sue Flowers. *Presence: Human Purpose and the Field of the Future*. New York: Doubleday, 2004.

Sisoida, Rajendra, David B. Wolfe, and Jagdish N. Sheth. *Firms of Endearment: How World-Class Companies Profit from Passion and Purpose*. Upper Saddle River, NJ: Wharton School Publishing, 2007.

Tolle, Eckhart. *The Power of Now: A Guide to Spiritual Enlightenment*. Vancouver, BC, Canada: Namaste Publishing, 1999.

Tolstoy, Leo. *The Death of Ivan Ilyich*. 1886.

Twerski, Abraham J. *When Do the Good Things Start? A Therapist Looks at Life's Ups and Downs (With a Bit of Help from Charlie Brown and His Friends)*. West Sussex, UK: Ravette Books Ltd., 1988.

ABOUT THE AUTHOR

Author Federico Renzo Grayeb has held leadership positions in major pharmaceutical companies in Europe, the United States, and Latin America. He has more than twenty years of experience turning around businesses by improving the working climate. Grayeb served as general manager of Novo Nordisk in Argentina, which was selected as the Best Company To Work For in 2003 and remained in the top five over the following four years under Grayeb's watch. Since 2007, he has overseen the Latin American operations of Novo Nordisk from Brazil, also recognized as one of the best companies to work for in that area. He is a founding member of Conscious Capitalism Brazil.

www.ingramcontent.com/pod-product-compliance
Lightning Source LLC
Chambersburg PA
CBHW021410170526
45164CB00002B/581